TRUMP SHALL NEVER DIE

HS PRESS

TRUMP SHALL NEVER DIE

His Determination to Come Back

RYUHO OKAWA

HS PRESS

No statements made by the guardian spirit of Mr. Donald Trump in this book reflect statements actually made by Mr. Donald Trump himself.

The opinions of the spirit do not necessarily reflect those of Happy Science Group. For the mechanism behind spiritual messages, see the end section.

Contents

CHAPTER ONE

Trump Shall Never Die
America Forever

CHAPTER TWO

The Determination to Come Back

For the Realization of World Justice

3 The Change in Administration Will Divide America

Afterword 173

Preface

This is a spiritual message from the guardian spirit of Mr. Trump, the former president of the United States. It is difficult even for the Japanese media to directly interview Mr. Trump who has now retreated to Florida. So, this book is a valuable primary source on him.

Mr. Trump may have made too many enemies because he was an unconventional president. But his uncommon, unpredictable actions surely worked to bring stability and safety in Asia and the Pacific region.

Ever since Mr. Biden was announced as the winner, many incidents—including the growing uncertainty of North Korea, China's implementation of hard-line policies on Hong Kong and increasing pressures on Taiwan, and the military coup d'état in Myanmar (Burma)—have occurred in just a few months. Also, the WHO research team was easily driven out of Wuhan.

"Trump shall never die"—people's call for Mr. Trump will grow louder by the end of this year.

Ryuho Okawa
Master & CEO of Happy Science Group
March 17, 2021

CHAPTER ONE

Trump Shall Never Die
America Forever

Originally recorded in Japanese on February 18, 2021
in the Special Lecture Hall of Happy Science in Japan
and later translated into English.

Donald Trump (1946 - Present)

An American politician and businessman. The 45th president of the United States. Republican. Born in New York City. After graduating from the University of Pennsylvania in 1968, he worked at a real estate company that his father was running and became its president in 1971. In 1983, he built the Trump Tower, known as the "world's most luxurious building" on Fifth Avenue in New York. He succeeded in real estate development and hotel and casino management. On January 20, 2017, he was inaugurated as the 45th president of the U.S. He ran for the 2020 presidential election for his second term but lost despite winning nearly half the votes.

Interviewers from Happy Science[*]

Shio Okawa
   Aide to Master & CEO

The Background That Led to This Spiritual Message

On February 18, 2021, Mr. Trump's guardian spirit came
to Master Ryuho Okawa to give a spiritual message.

1

How Mr. Trump Sees
the New President Biden

Mr. Trump's current state of mind
after the impeachment trial

[*Editor's Note: The original song by Master Ryuho Okawa, "Waruiko wa Inai-ka? – Kusatsu Akaoni-san no Uta –" (lit., "Any bad kids? – Song of the Kusatsu Red Ogre –") is playing in the background.*]

DONALD TRUMP'S GUARDIAN SPIRIT
Umm, ah. I'm Donald Trump.

SHIO OKAWA
Oh, it's (the guardian spirit of) Mr. Trump.

TRUMP'S G.S.
It takes quite a lot of time and energy to make a book with just one (recording) session, so could you record my

spiritual message here, just briefly? I'm afraid I'm doing the same thing as (the guardian spirit of) Biden (see p. 201), but I'm sure it'll make things easier for you later on.

SHIO OKAWA
I understand.

TRUMP'S G.S.
Yes. I don't mind if you are the only one (interviewer). I respect Mrs. Shio Okawa very much.

SHIO OKAWA
Thank you very much. Since you're here, please go ahead (and start your spiritual message).

TRUMP'S G.S.
It seems like this is family time, so maybe the "president" shouldn't have come. Perhaps I'm bothering you.

SHIO OKAWA
Not at all.

TRUMP'S G.S.

[*Glances at Master Ryuho Okawa's grandson.*] Huh? You don't mind? I probably look like a red ogre. I feel bad. [*As he sees the grandson leaving the room.*] Oh no, the cute boy has been "repelled." I'm a red ogre after all.

Here comes the red ogre of America♪ I'm sorry for your grandson♪

SHIO OKAWA

No, that's all right. How are you doing, Mr. Trump? The impeachment trial ended.

TRUMP'S G.S.

I cleared it for now, but a country or a national system that tries to make an innocent man a criminal is completely wrong. The country is trying to make a national hero a criminal, so he would never be able to get up again. From the perspective of justice, we need to turn this situation around.

SHIO OKAWA

Right.

TRUMP'S G.S.

It's a bit frustrating.

Describing Mr. Biden as an average person

SHIO OKAWA

Listening to Mr. Biden's guardian spirit, he seems...

TRUMP'S G.S.

Vague.

SHIO OKAWA

...he's trying to wreak his grudge against you...

TRUMP'S G.S.

That's right.

SHIO OKAWA

...out of his personal feelings.

TRUMP'S G.S.

He's persistent, isn't he?

SHIO OKAWA

Yes. Stubborn.

TRUMP'S G.S.

It's not that he got a high position because he was capable. He floated around like air and buttered up to people. He served somebody younger than him, and as he curried favors with women and black people, he stood in power before he knew it. When the bad people were "removed," he was left. He needs to be careful; his luck could drag him to hell.

SHIO OKAWA

Also, he probably has the tendency to pull strings from behind (based on what I heard from his spiritual messages).

TRUMP'S G.S.

That means he's just an average person. Average people do those things. There aren't people like me who can squarely fight the mass media by calling them fake news and continue serving as president. Nobody has such mental strength.

SHIO OKAWA

You must be tough to do that.

TRUMP'S G.S.

You can't unless you're tough.

I guess the media can't properly evaluate me. They chose an ordinary guy that they can easily manipulate and are trying to control him, right? They're trying to use somebody who will do as he's told.

Can Mr. Biden take responsibility for the possible side effects of coronavirus vaccines?

TRUMP'S G.S.

They're making it look like they're off to a good start, but people will gradually start to complain. To begin with, Biden's presidency depends greatly on Pfizer's...

SHIO OKAWA

Vaccines?

TRUMP'S G.S.

...vaccines being mass-produced, everybody getting the vaccines, and the coronavirus completely disappearing. Then, he's going to say, "See! As soon as I became president,

I responded to this issue quickly and saved so many lives." And he thinks his name will go down in history just for that.

But I'm saying, "It's not *you* who saved people." The vaccine would've become available even if I were re-elected.

SHIO OKAWA
Right.

TRUMP'S G.S.
The vaccines weren't completed while I was in office because the pharmaceutical companies held back. If they had announced the completion of the vaccines while I was in office, the election results could've been different.

There's nothing we can do about the virus, you know? It spreads through the air. We're not sure if the vaccine will even work.

Biden will have to take responsibility for the effectiveness of the pharmaceutical companies' vaccines. Even if they're effective for Americans, there's no telling whether they will be equally effective for Japanese people. There have already been reports about the side effects, but those vaccines will certainly have side effects. I'm afraid many people will die in different ways. I wonder if he can take responsibility. It'll be tough.

If 100 million people are vaccinated and 1 percent of them suffer from side effects, that would be 1 million people, right?

SHIO OKAWA
That's right.

TRUMP'S G.S.
Even 0.1 percent of them will be 100,000 people. It'll be tough. He won't be able to take responsibility.

People making the vaccines are rushing their jobs. They're taking random samples of the coronavirus from various people, mixing something like "egg whites" into them, and mass-producing the vaccines. Nobody can tell whether they will really work or not.

But people who die from taking a vaccine shot will probably die without it anyway. They'll probably die easily.

"Trump supporters no longer have freedom of the press, and they're being silenced"

TRUMP'S G.S.

I wanted people to put aside these things and understand what I had done.

SHIO OKAWA

Do you mean the American people and people around the world?

TRUMP'S G.S.

You know, I was just hated by certain groups of people. I was only applauded when Melania appeared in a bold outfit.

SHIO OKAWA

But in those circumstances, nearly 75 million people voted for Mr. Trump, so I'm sure there are people who understand you.

TRUMP'S G.S.

But they're being silenced. Those people no longer have freedom of the press.

SHIO OKAWA

They're now being called crazy, fanatic, and blind believers, or brainwashed people.

TRUMP'S G.S.

Yes, that's right. If you take radical action, you're called a fanatic. I'm rather like an X-MEN. They think I'm a mutant. People think I'm some kind of mutant president born in America. They think I might transform from Trump into a giant bear and go on a rampage.

It's a little frustrating. Why can't they understand me?

"Let's see what Biden can do about China, Iran, and other issues"

TRUMP'S G.S.

China will first taunt Biden to test the waters. They're watching what he'll do with Myanmar and Iran. Let's see if he can do anything other than "peace at any price." China is also watching what he'll do with Israel.

A world without a leader will probably continue. Even if you ask Biden a question, he'll just tell you to ask the person in charge of that. He'll tell you that it's up to the cabinet members to decide because he doesn't have his own opinion. So, you know...

I wonder what he'll do about issues with Iran, China, Russia, and Myanmar—I mean, Burma.

2

The Prospects of Coronavirus Vaccines and the Tokyo Olympic Games

"The vaccines won't work, but instead lower your immunity"

TRUMP'S G.S.

It'll probably take a year to find out whether the vaccine works or not. He can buy time while the vaccines are being shot. It's the only thing he can do.

Japan is just about starting to give the vaccine to the public, right? I'm afraid some bad things will happen.

SHIO OKAWA

You mean side effects?

TRUMP'S G.S.

Healthcare workers will receive the shots and soon complain that they're feeling ill, which will accelerate the collapse of the healthcare system.

SHIO OKAWA

There are also mutated coronavirus strains.

TRUMP'S G.S.

The vaccine doesn't work much in the first place. It depends on how you look at it. If you think it's effective, it'll work. If you don't think it works, it won't. Older people and those with underlying medical problems would die from getting pneumonia, and those who would die from a bad cold—I mean the flu—would also die from the coronavirus. So, even with the vaccine, those who will die will die.

SHIO OKAWA

That may be true. People with lower immunity and declining health are in danger the most.

TRUMP'S G.S.

You're injecting something bad into the body to develop immunity to it. If it works, it's good, but if it doesn't... It's like injecting the flu virus, so it's terrible.

I think a vaccine is effective if you get the shot before the disease spreads, but not very effective if the disease has already spread. Everybody has been infected with various types of the coronavirus already, including a mild case. There are mild, moderate, and severe cases, but most people already have the virus. It probably doesn't mean much to get vaccine shots in such a situation. People are fighting the mild case of coronavirus and if they win, they survive; if they get worse, they end up in hospitals.

The vaccination is a ceremony just for show to make it appear as if the president saved the lives of his people. But in reality, he can't save everybody.

The vaccines can't save Japanese people, either. Now, the number of new coronavirus cases in Japan has reduced so much, with 200 to 300 in Tokyo and a little over 100 in Osaka (at the time of the spiritual message). You don't need vaccines in such a situation. You shouldn't get vaccine shots. The virus will disappear naturally. That's the safest way.

The government is trying to get people vaccinated and infected. But what is the point in infecting all 100 million Japanese people and developing their immunity? The coronavirus vaccine includes the DNA of the AIDS virus, so the vaccine will likely work to lower your immunity and make it easier for you to contract various diseases.

Well, I won't deny the effect of the vaccines. There's nothing else they can do for now. But I think the government is trying to pass the buck to healthcare workers by encouraging people to get vaccinated.

How Mr. Trump sees media reports of Japanese politicians drinking out at night or attending parties

TRUMP'S G.S.

Also, I felt a sense of danger when I saw the media reporting that Japanese politicians are resigning or leaving the Liberal Democratic Party just because they were drinking out at night or attending parties. Japan is like a country made of glass. It's dangerous.

Your (country's) opinions depend on the articles of the mere weekly magazines? The major newspapers (in Japan) aren't brave enough to write about the country's problems, so they have weekly magazines write about them first, and then write their own articles afterward. That's how they increase their circulations.

SHIO OKAWA

But the ones taking those photos are also outside at that time of night.

TRUMP'S G.S.

Right. So, they aren't following the state of emergency orders either, and are hiding out at night. They, too, might be drinking with those politicians. They are bat-like people who are active at night.

SHIO OKAWA

These politicians were trying to penalize the people in the first place. If they try to penalize the public, it's natural that they should also be penalized.

TRUMP'S G.S.

Those politicians and top bureaucrats are saying, "You, ignorant people, just obey us and follow our orders." It is necessary to get rid of those people, so in that sense, it was good that they resigned.

Those who were trying to impose penalties on the public over coronavirus matters are all "fired" now, after it was revealed they themselves were not abiding by the rules. Next is the Olympics. The people who are trying to host the Olympics will be "gone" soon.

Views on the Tokyo Olympics and the Winter Olympics in China

TRUMP'S G.S.

Japan can go ahead with the Olympics, but looking at what's going on in the world now, with so many people infected, dying, and with hospitals overwhelmed, this is not the right time, to be honest. This is not peacetime.

In wartime, you shouldn't be holding the Olympics. You shouldn't casually invite the people of the country that is trying to establish hegemony and start a war, and broadcast the games.

China is also trying to hold the Winter Olympics, right? Supporting them would be similar to supporting Hitler.

3

America Must Establish World Justice

"Mediocre people staged a coup d'état against me, but I won't let it end like this"

SHIO OKAWA

The other day, we recorded a spiritual message from the guardian spirit of Mr. Xi Jinping (see p. 200). It seemed like something other than Mr. Xi Jinping's own soul has entered his body and is trying to plot something. We got the impression that he is becoming increasingly threatening. Now that Mr. Trump is no longer president, it seems that the darkness is growing even bigger in Mr. Xi Jinping.

TRUMP'S G.S.

That's right. He has started to make a move.

I had God's support on my side. The Light of El Cantare was shedding on the U.S. through God Thoth, and I was fighting following the words of Thoth. But the mediocre people who claimed those words from God to be unscientific and nonsensical staged a coup d'état against me and formed a new government.

But I won't let it end like this. OK? "Trump shall never die."

SHIO OKAWA
That's cool!

TRUMP'S G.S.
Let's use it as the title.

SHIO OKAWA & TRUMP'S G.S.
"Trump shall never die."

SHIO OKAWA
It's cool.

TRUMP'S G.S.
It's cool, isn't it? "Trump Forever." I like it.

SHIO OKAWA
I like it, too.

TRUMP'S G.S.

Ah, it sounds good.

SHIO OKAWA

It's nice.

"There was voter fraud in the election, but they went through with it"

TRUMP'S G.S.

So, you know, all these mediocre people got together and pretended to have won the election, but it's true that there were fake votes. Overturning the outcome of the election was too much a burden for them (the Supreme Court and Congress), so they went through with it.

SHIO OKAWA

I heard that plenty of ballots were sent to deceased people.

TRUMP'S G.S.

That's right. Millions of dead people had the "right" to vote, and somehow they voted. So, we should be asking, "Who did it?"

Votes can be bought. You can buy votes. They dared to do this kind of thing. I believe the election was rigged. But I guess they didn't want to overturn the election result because they thought it would bring confusion to the country.

"The new administration is cowardly, so they might not fight for Japan"

TRUMP'S G.S.
Well, that's fine. I won't say anything if things turn out for the better. If things get better in the end, then it's OK.

But the new administration is all bark and no bite. They pretend to keep America the way it has been, but they are actually cowardly and cannot do what must be done. I don't think it's a good idea to leave the country in the hands of such cowardly administration.

SHIO OKAWA
Also, after Mr. Trump's defeat, I feel that the U.S. is apt to be an even more atheist nation, or a Godless nation where

people are defeated by the virus. It feels like the U.S. is more and more leaning toward a materialistic way of thinking.

TRUMP'S G.S.

Well, the situation of the Uyghurs is hopeless now. The situation in Hong Kong is also hopeless because the pope won't protect them.

SHIO OKAWA

Taiwan must be getting nervous, too.

TRUMP'S G.S.

Taiwan needs to protect itself like a hedgehog. You know, people are saying a lot lately that China is trying to get the Pratas Islands, which Japan is not aware of, in addition to the Spratly Islands and Paracel Islands in the South China Sea. The Pratas Islands are small islands to the west of Taiwan. They are far away from Japan and cannot actually be seen from Japan. China has simulated a scenario of landing on and occupying them.

What would Japan do, if China suddenly lands on the Senkaku Islands, takes effective control over them, and quickly builds structures and artillery batteries? Will the U.S. fight for Japan? I'm not sure about that. It's hard to say. The current administration is cowardly, so they might not fight.

SHIO OKAWA

I think you're right. The Japanese government agreed to allocate the so-called "sympathy budget" for the U.S. military bases at an earlier stage and it appears as though the U.S. will protect Japan, but it's doubtful whether they'll actually fight for Japan.

"Don't let political decision-makers and perpetrators who spread the coronavirus get away"

TRUMP'S G.S.

At least, regarding the coronavirus pandemic, I believe that the perpetrators who actually spread the coronavirus globally were definitely Chinese. That's how I see it. These people must be arrested, or if not, we must at least attack China's strategic locations. Otherwise, we won't be able to establish world justice.

There are more than 100 million infected people in countries all over the world, and the number continues to grow. Their (China's) leadership must be put in prison for spreading the virus.

SHIO OKAWA
Mr. Biden's guardian spirit said that even so, the U.S. was jointly developing the coronavirus with China in the beginning, so if they pursue China's responsibility, it will also point back to the U.S. That's why they don't want to do it.

TRUMP'S G.S.
Those are just excuses. Everything he says is an excuse. It's true that China tried to steal American technology. They tried to steal American genetic engineering technology. But science alone cannot decide how this scientific technology is used. It's politics that decides how the technology is used. So, politics is held accountable for making decisions. We must thoroughly investigate them about this point.

Scientists will do all kinds of research if they are free to do what they want. American technology is advanced, so there are people who came from China to study in the U.S. and stole technology by pretending to be a co-researcher. But American scientists refused to cooperate when a foreign government maliciously intervened and tried to misuse the technology. This shows the conscience of the U.S.

Anyway, regarding this pandemic, China must have spread the virus intentionally. It doesn't take many people to do it, so it must have been done by the special operations forces of the People's Liberation Army. They must be identified. They are communicating with each other through an electronic network, so in order to get evidence of this chain of command, we just need to keep track of it. We will definitely be able to find evidence this way. The evidence will definitely come out. I think this should be brought forth.

The people who were involved in this must be arrested and the U.S. must never forgive the ones who gave the orders and directions to spread the virus. The U.S. must maintain this attitude regardless of the money we make from our trade with China. We will not tolerate an evil empire. We will not allow it to flourish. We will protect world justice. America is Superman. America is the country of Superman. We can't compromise this.

Don't be fooled by Biden's excuse to get himself out of responsibility. By saying that the U.S. may have been an accomplice, he's trying to discourage the Americans from investigating China (for spreading the coronavirus), but don't fall for this trick. This is "average Joe's wisdom."

SHIO OKAWA
I see.

TRUMP'S G.S.
The more cowardly you are, the better you are at making excuses. So, we'd better be careful. I'm saying, "Leaving aside the researchers, don't let people who made political decisions and others who actually spread the virus get away." I will never forgive them.

"The head of WHO should be fired and made to confess in public"

SHIO OKAWA
Americans stopped the joint research at some point, which means that their conscience was at work.

TRUMP'S G.S.
That's right.

SHIO OKAWA
So, whether a country has conscience or not, whether it can put a stop on itself, will also decide whether it is allowed to be a hegemonic country.

TRUMP'S G.S.
We know that China conducted their research on the virus, but we don't have any evidence now. The WHO went to Wuhan a year later and reported that they didn't find anything. Really, they just proved their own stupidity again and went home. And Biden said the U.S. is rejoining the WHO, right? This is just foolish. The head of the WHO must be fired and made to confess in public.

You know, if China had the most... It would make sense if 100 million Chinese got infected and the disease spread to the rest of the world, infecting tens of millions in the U.S. But while the number of infected people hasn't increased in China, it has only increased in America and Europe. How can there be such a virus? It's absolutely impossible.

SHIO OKAWA

Yes, it's strange.

TRUMP'S G.S.

It just isn't possible. There's definitely somebody who brought it in and spread it.

Objecting against Mr. Biden's attempt to replace the coronavirus issue with human rights issues

TRUMP'S G.S.

What's more, the virus works even on Indian people. This means that China has done a lot of research. There is no way that Indians are more vulnerable to germs than the Chinese. They are strong. They eat rice by mixing it with their bare hands. Can you eat curry and rice with your sanitized hands? I don't think so.

They don't have the habit of using a spoon, and such strong people are getting infected. So, there must be somebody who spread the virus. Somebody with significant decision-making power must be behind this. We have to make this clear, and we have to cooperate with the international community to reveal this.

He (Biden) changes the topic slightly and says that we should work together with the international community to solve the human rights issues in China. But it's almost as good as saying that he'll do nothing. He says that the U.S. will cooperate with Japan, Australia, New Zealand, and the U.K. to tackle these issues, but his way of making himself look good in this way is basically the way of the Democrats.

SHIO OKAWA
In America, calling the virus "Wuhan virus" or "China virus" was banned because these terms lead to the discrimination against Chinese people and other Asian people.

TRUMP'S G.S.
But if they're doing something bad, they can't avoid being discriminated against.

SHIO OKAWA
It's customary to name a disease after the place it originated, such as the Spanish flu.

TRUMP'S G.S.

It's not the New York virus.

SHIO OKAWA

No, it's not. People say terms like the "Wuhan virus" and "China virus" shouldn't be used, but this is actually one of the most important points of discussion.

TRUMP'S G.S.

The enemy will take advantage of this weak attitude.

Well, Japan might also... If Biden tells Japan to join hands, it'll most probably mean he won't be doing anything at all. He isn't really thinking about anything.

SHIO OKAWA

He thinks quite similarly to how the Japanese do.

TRUMP'S G.S.

Doesn't he? If he asks Japan to join the human rights diplomacy for Asia, it's as good as saying he would do nothing.

SHIO OKAWA

He might say that because it sounds nice.

TRUMP'S G.S.

Nobody will be able to oppose him if he says so. No way.

SHIO OKAWA

I hope you will live long.

TRUMP'S G.S.

Well, even after four years, I'll still be Biden's age now.

SHIO OKAWA

So, there'll be no problem.

TRUMP'S G.S.

I'll be OK. Even at 80 years old, I think I'll still have the energy to make children. I don't drink much.

SHIO OKAWA

That's true.

TRUMP'S G.S.

I don't eat or drink anything bad, you know. My body is "Superman." Yes, "Trump shall never die."

4

"America Will Be Back Again"

"There are only two gods of America: Washington and Lincoln"

SHIO OKAWA

Do you spiritually communicate with President Lincoln?

TRUMP'S G.S.

Of course I do.

SHIO OKAWA

I thought so.

TRUMP'S G.S.

There are only two gods of America: Washington and Lincoln. Others are just helping these gods. There are only two gods. These gods must essentially be under the direct command of the true God of the Earth.

"The important thing is to establish world justice"

TRUMP'S G.S.

It's very frustrating to have been taken over by mediocre people and the mass media created by average people, and to have allowed them to flip values. But I believe we can change the tide again within a year.

I want to keep saying that the flame of truth will never be distinguished. I want to build up my strength in Florida for another comeback. I have already collected a decent amount of funds for the next election campaign, so we are able to carry out our activities.

Biden will show his true colors. I'm sure he will. He will expose his faults within a year. That's when we will go on the offensive.

SHIO OKAWA

I believe the law of cause and effect works in this world as well, so your righteousness will be proven one day.

TRUMP'S G.S.

We're not Reptilians, you know? We're not belligerent. We don't enjoy killing or discriminating against people.

The important thing is to establish world justice. It doesn't matter whether the culprits are white, black, or yellow.

SHIO OKAWA
No, it doesn't.

TRUMP'S G.S.
Not at all. What matters is whether a person's thoughts and beliefs are doing harm to the world.

SHIO OKAWA
Yes, exactly. It's the people who bring up race in these issues that are discriminating people by race.

Proactive diplomacy is needed in this time of growing risk of a new war

TRUMP'S G.S.
Now, I feel the same as Batman, who takes the blame and hides himself. That's how I feel.

SHIO OKAWA

You mean, "Not yet."

TRUMP'S G.S.

Not yet. This is not the end. America is not over. Not yet. As long as I'm alive, America is not over. Even if Biden is alive, America is not over as long as I'm alive. I have no intention of making America a "banal" nation. I will never allow dictators to emerge one after another (in the world).

SHIO OKAWA

When we recorded the spiritual message of (the guardian spirit of) Xi Jinping after you stepped down, I felt the darkness was growing deeper in him.

TRUMP'S G.S.

Yes.

SHIO OKAWA

I also realized that Mr. Trump had a great influence, after all.

TRUMP'S G.S.

Now in Myanmar... or Burma, its democratic system is about to be overturned by the military. I think the same will happen in the Middle East. The U.S. is said to be returning to the six-party talks, but Iran has already started to develop nuclear weapons again. Israel has also started to prepare for a nuclear war because it has lost the backing of the U.S. It is going to fight on its own. So, the risk of a new war is there.

SHIO OKAWA

You mean, the risk is growing.

TRUMP'S G.S.

Yes, it is. It's unfortunate.

It might be hard to believe, but even a leader like Putin trusts what Trump says. He doesn't trust what Biden says because Biden breaks his promises. So, there's no point in making promises with him. I think Putin has been thinking a lot.

We need proactive diplomacy. We had enough fine talk. Go back (to Africa) and continue it with the Dogons.

SHIO OKAWA

Right. There is nothing wrong with using such nice words if he actually solves problems.

TRUMP'S G.S.

So, I really want to say, "Not yet." We still have a lot to do. We must fight.

In the worst-case scenario, you must fly out with a neutron bomb (as depicted in the movie, *The Dark Knight Rises*). That's how the president of the United States should be.

Some people may be thinking I'm dead, but I'm not. Trump's not dead.

SHIO OKAWA

No, you're not!

"I want to create an opportunity for a counterattack within a year"

TRUMP'S G.S.

Trump will make a comeback, definitely. Now, people are treated as insane if they support Trump, you know?

SHIO OKAWA

That's sad.

TRUMP'S G.S.

That's true in the U.S., in Japan, and in the world. So, they have no choice but to lie low for now.

SHIO OKAWA

That's not good.

TRUMP'S G.S.

It's like the Red Scare in the old days. Just like McCarthyism back then, the "Trump Scare" is going on now. People who speak well of Trump or speak friendly of Trump will be "hunted."

SHIO OKAWA

That's rude.

TRUMP'S G.S.

Biden says that he will get rid of division and unify the country, and build a country where its people get along with each other, but that's not true at all.

SHIO OKAWA

So, you mean labeling people as insane works to divide the country? You're right, indeed.

TRUMP'S G.S.

I can only think that they (Democrats) are taking advantage of their enemy's missteps, so that they can take over the country themselves, all at once.

So, I want to create an opportunity for a counterattack within a year, and we want to regain power around the next midterm elections. We can still make a comeback in Congress.

"We need to have our own media because we can't trust GAFA"

TRUMP'S G.S.

Also, we should bring back conservative media. We must have our own media because we can't trust GAFA anymore.

SHIO OKAWA

Really, I know.

TRUMP'S G.S.

We can't trust them. Nobody knows how much "China profit" has infiltrated those companies.

You should be careful, too. I'm serious. Major companies like GAFA act only for their own benefit, not for justice. They act only to make a profit. You have to be careful, seriously.

SHIO OKAWA

They started to filter information quite heavily. It's no longer objective.

"Don't be misled by environmental issues"

TRUMP'S G.S.

The environmental issue is another problem. This "guru-less" issue, of which Greta is becoming the "guru," is a very unscientific matter, I think. It's dangerous. We have to be careful. I'm serious.

In Japan, people suffer from cold weather and heavy snow. It's so cold that I'm getting a stuffy nose as I talk. How can you generate solar power under these circumstances? You can't rely on it in areas that snow heavily like this. In areas where the wind blows strongly, wind power generation is promoted, but it's not stable, either.

Nuclear power generation is reconsidered in Japan because there are many earthquakes, but China has been constructing a lot of nuclear power plants, as well as coal and oil power plants. They keep constructing them and they don't care about the environment. They are egoists. They emit CO_2 like crazy.

When China says that they will stop using oil by 2060, it means that they will start thinking about it in 2059. They can produce all kinds of fake statistics. They can fabricate data as much as they want to look as though CO_2 emissions have been reduced. So, they can't be trusted.

What's more, I'm afraid China will also steal marine resources both in the Sea of Japan and the Pacific Ocean. So, the day will come when Japanese people won't be able to eat fish. China is sending their tourists to Japan, but their aim is to make Japanese people speak Chinese. You, Japanese people, are too nice, so you have to be careful. You should study English harder and do business with Chinese people in English. You shouldn't do much business in Chinese because that's what they want.

"There is no political science in China, they only teach people their justified history"

TRUMP'S G.S.

China is thinking of something extremely evil. Their aim is world domination. It's an invasion.

SHIO OKAWA

They are thinking of far more evil things than what ordinary people think of.

TRUMP'S G.S.

Yes, they are.

SHIO OKAWA

That's why most people can't believe what China is actually thinking about.

TRUMP'S G.S.

That's because people believe China is a democratic nation. But even their universities are completely brainwashed. Universities are unified under the Mao Zedong thought or Xi Jinping thought. There is no political science in China, basically. They just teach people their justified history.

When the Chinese come to study in Japan, their government doesn't allow them to study political science or law, but only economics, right? Not so many Chinese students come to Japan, though.

Also, China is aiming to steal technology from the West because they think Western technology is more advanced.

You know, I'm not sure if Japanese people can fulfill their true mission, considering the weak Japanese political system now.

"Without justice, the U.S. will be nothing but a moneymaker"

TRUMP'S G.S.

Anyway, I will make a comeback somehow. I think Happy Science will come up too, if you support me.

When it comes to the information on space people, I'm not sure how much Biden will disclose.

SHIO OKAWA

Exactly.

TRUMP'S G.S.

He probably doesn't want such beings to exist because that will make the American people anxious.

Biden thinks very similarly to the Japanese, so be careful.

SHIO OKAWA

May God's justice be realized on earth.

TRUMP'S G.S.

Yes. A god will surely strike back even if he appears to have retreated temporarily. He is now devising strategies to do so. America will be back again.

If necessary, I'll have Ivanka fight on behalf of me.

SHIO OKAWA
That might work, too.

TRUMP'S G.S.
I'll consider having Ivanka run for the presidency if the black vice president will run for the president. America will not lose.

SHIO OKAWA
Justice of the true God is full of love for humanity.

TRUMP'S G.S.
Of course.

SHIO OKAWA
I really believe so.

TRUMP'S G.S.

Without justice, the U.S. will be nothing but a moneymaker. It's not good.

We will enter the space age from now on. So, we will also need "space justice." Only Master Ryuho Okawa of Happy Science teaches it now. So, I want America to be a nation that can support Happy Science as well.

SHIO OKAWA

Thank you very much.

TRUMP'S G.S.

The pope won't protect you. He doesn't even protect Christians. He has forsaken them. The pope has given up on the Christians in China and Hong Kong. He has feelings against the U.S., so he won't save Americans, either. Then, will South America become rich? I don't see that happening.

To choose something, you must give up something. It means you can distinguish between right and wrong.

SHIO OKAWA

Yes, you're right.

"Trump shall never die" "America Forever"

TRUMP'S G.S.

I shouldn't talk too much. Today's session is just a prologue of a book.

SHIO OKAWA

An introduction...

TRUMP'S G.S.

Oh, yes, yes.

SHIO OKAWA

This is just an introduction, but the title has been decided.

TRUMP'S G.S.

We shouldn't imitate Biden, but... You know what? It's about time for us to counterattack. The next counterpunch.

SHIO OKAWA

"Trump shall never die."

TRUMP'S G.S.

"Trump shall never die," yes.

SHIO OKAWA

It's a cool title.

TRUMP'S G.S.

"America Forever."

SHIO OKAWA

It sounds good.

TRUMP'S G.S.

I am the Batman for America.

5

A Secret Plan for a Trump Comeback

"Biden, who knows nothing about making money in business, will accept money under the table"

SHIO OKAWA

[*To Interviewer A*] Is there anything you want to ask?

TRUMP'S G.S.

Do you have any questions?

INTERVIEWER A

Do you have any secret plan to make a comeback within a year?

TRUMP'S G.S.

Biden is an "average Joe," so he will make a blunder.

A

Do you mean that you are waiting for him to trip up?

TRUMP'S G.S.

The mass media has lost their... They've gone crazy. It'll take a little while for them to calm down.

There's nothing I can do for now, so I'll wait in Florida until the time is right. Biden is probably thinking of removing the Trump Tower from New York. I think so.

SHIO OKAWA

I remember his guardian spirit saying so in his spiritual message the other day.

TRUMP'S G.S.

He really is.

SHIO OKAWA

He probably wants to go that far.

TRUMP'S G.S.

He might be thinking of destroying us by raising taxes, but it's not that easy.

SHIO OKAWA

He has a lot of other problems he must think about.

TRUMP'S G.S.

He has never worked as a businessperson, so... He has no idea. He doesn't know what business is all about.

It'll be a government full of corruption again. He'll accept money from all kinds of people. After all, he doesn't know how to make money through business.

SHIO OKAWA

Oh, that's true.

TRUMP'S G.S.

He accepts money under the table.

SHIO OKAWA

He (guardian spirit) said something like, "It's good to receive money."

TRUMP'S G.S.

Yes, that's right. He receives money, saying, "You guys are supporting my politics, huh?"

SHIO OKAWA

He thinks it's not a bad thing for rich people to give him money.

TRUMP'S G.S.

Japan needs a "new power," you know? There are a lot of bad things in Japan, especially the "Chinalized" parts. So, you need to fire yourselves up more (as a new power).

Expectations for Ivanka and her husband Jared Kushner

SHIO OKAWA

In your eyes, does Ivanka share your sense of justice?

TRUMP'S G.S.

She's brilliant.

SHIO OKAWA

I see. I thought so.

TRUMP'S G.S.

Ivanka is brilliant. She's smart, has a great temperament, and is a great decision-maker. I'd marry her if she wasn't my daughter.

SHIO OKAWA

Really?

A

Your surface consciousness (Trump himself) said the same thing.

TRUMP'S G.S.

We're trying to figure out a way to make a Jewish person the president.

SHIO OKAWA

So, she takes after your way of thinking and your thoughts on God's justice.

TRUMP'S G.S.

Kushner is pretty brilliant too, you know. Far better than Biden. He has very good practical business capabilities.

SHIO OKAWA

I heard that before he married your daughter, he was good enough to go head-to-head with you. That was before you became the president.

TRUMP'S G.S.

Good enough to be my rival in the real estate industry. He's no less than Biden. The couple—both of them—has a good chance of running for president.

A

I guess the only thing to consider is that they are both Jewish.

TRUMP'S G.S.

I'm considering bringing it up, depending on how things go, because we need to take revenge politically. But I haven't brought it up yet because I'm thinking of giving it another shot myself. There are still things I must do. But if people say I can't be the president at Biden's age, then so be it. I'll pass it on to her generation.

"It's the American mission to protect the world"

TRUMP'S G.S.

The American spirit is not dead. It's the American mission to protect the world.

SHIO OKAWA

Age means nothing to a person with the mission and ability to serve many people.

TRUMP'S G.S.

Master Okawa is a little younger than me, so I'm sure he'll work longer.

I want you to spread that spirit in Japan, too, as our ally. It's important that Japan sends out opinions. Don't blindly accept what the U.S. media says. It's encouraging just to know that there are people who don't blindly accept what they say. Your support reaches me in many ways. So, I'm counting on you. Keep going.

SHIO OKAWA

Thank you.

TRUMP'S G.S.

It's not that I hate Iran. I believe we have to prevent a nuclear war from occurring in the Middle East. To the people of different ethnic groups there, it might be a matter of "happy or unhappy," or "fair or unfair," but I think we should defang Iran to make sure they don't start a nuclear war in the Middle East.

Negotiations in which China participates are no good at all. Those don't count. The UN should be reformed, too. The permanent members of the Security Council should be reconsidered. Countries that don't share the same values shouldn't be allowed as permanent members.

The UN is just an empty shell. It's powerless. It's just a waste of money. The UN Forces won't be able to function if the UN stays as it is. The UN should be reformed, so that those with shared values are able to work together.

Countermeasures against China, which has made money one-sidedly from its trade with the U.S.

TRUMP'S G.S.
It's highly likely that everything will be mixed up under Biden.

SHIO OKAWA
You mean that he has little idea of what's right and wrong?

TRUMP'S G.S.

He can't take action. Not with the way he is now.

A

He reminds me of Japanese politicians.

SHIO OKAWA

You're right, they're very similar.

TRUMP'S G.S.

They probably think it's enough to just get along with every country.

SHIO OKAWA

Yes, yes. Exactly.

TRUMP'S G.S.

It's not enough.

SHIO OKAWA

They think as long as they get along with every country without stirring up any trouble, they won't suffer damages during their administration.

TRUMP'S G.S.

With the coronavirus relief spending, the U.S. now has a massive budget deficit. To solve this issue, the Biden administration will probably try to tax people of higher income.

But instead, they should "squeeze" money out of the country that made money from its trade with the U.S. Actually, it's not "squeezing," it's "having them give us in return." It has to be a fair trade. Some of the money China made one-sidedly off of the U.S. should be returned. The U.S. should take responsibility and crush China's economic bubble.

So, you know... I'd like to believe that the time will come when people need me again. If not, my daughter and her husband will fight with a sense of responsibility on behalf of me.

SHIO OKAWA

Right. We're praying for you. We're praying that you will live long.

A

Yes, we pray that you will.

TRUMP'S G.S.
Thank you. Please don't forget me. It wouldn't be good to title the book, *Goodbye, Trump*.

SHIO OKAWA
No, it wouldn't.

TRUMP'S G.S.
No. Make sure to give it a different title.

SHIO OKAWA
It'll be, *Trump Shall Never Die*.

TRUMP'S G.S.
That's good. OK.

"Many black people were hired as police officers and military personnel during my presidency"

TRUMP'S G.S.
People might see you (Happy Science) as a far-right group, but you guys are saying the right thing.

Now, Trump supporters are considered fanatics or people with blind faith. They're treated as if they were the KKK, you know, with the white outfit.

SHIO OKAWA

Right. To me, it only seems that the people against you are depriving you and your supporters of the freedom of speech or expression.

TRUMP'S G.S.

Many black people were hired as police officers and military personnel during my presidency, so I don't deserve to be criticized like that.

SHIO OKAWA

You're right. Even in the protests that began from the death of a black person, a lot of people were killed.

TRUMP'S G.S.

Exactly.

SHIO OKAWA

Killed, in the riots they claim to be "protests."

TRUMP'S G.S.
That's right.

SHIO OKAWA
But no one criticizes that. They only bombard your side with criticisms, accusing you and your supporters of being racists or crazed rioters. It's not fair.

TRUMP'S G.S.
No.

"People who don't believe in God only have the desire to multiply themselves"

TRUMP'S G.S.
And while Biden is in power, China is using Huawei and others that we tried to get rid of, to take over Asia. We need a strategic plan against this.

SHIO OKAWA
You're right.

TRUMP'S G.S.

Something similar is going on in Myanmar, most likely. China is already starting to take over Myanmar.

A

Do you think China had something to do with the coup d'état in Myanmar?

TRUMP'S G.S.

Soon, it will happen in Thailand, too. China intends to conquer Asia. They are also going to occupy all the oil regions and then say, "CO_2? We'll think about it later."

SHIO OKAWA

It amazes me that they can be so greedy. Are they dying to have the Earth only for themselves?

TRUMP'S G.S.

People who don't believe in God only have the desire to multiply themselves. It's the same as the coronavirus. Just multiplying themselves.

SHIO OKAWA

Wow.

TRUMP'S G.S.

There is a lot we have to fight against.

"I struck my first blow.
Trump will definitely come back!"

TRUMP'S G.S.

Today was just an "opening act."

SHIO OKAWA

Right.

TRUMP'S G.S.

Did I speak for about 40 minutes?

SHIO OKAWA

Actually, 44 minutes.

TRUMP'S G.S.

Oh. Well, it was enough as a prologue, I guess.

SHIO OKAWA

Yes. Let's record a formal one next time.

TRUMP'S G.S.

Yes. You can ask me about something more specific, I mean, about my strategies.

SHIO OKAWA

OK. Thank you.

TRUMP'S G.S.

I struck my first blow. Trump will definitely come back!

SHIO OKAWA

This will light the candle of hope in many people.

TRUMP'S G.S.

Yes, yes. That's right.

I don't think the Japanese mass media fully trust Biden yet. Right now, the Japanese people only care about whether the vaccine will work or not. Whether Prime Minister Suga can stay in power depends solely on that, right? I feel sorry for him, but what he sees is too small. So, we need to talk about the bigger picture.

SHIO OKAWA
Right. Thank you very much.

A
Thank you very much.

TRUMP'S G.S.
Sure.

RYUHO OKAWA
[*Claps twice.*]

CHAPTER TWO

The Determination to Come Back

For the Realization of World Justice

*Originally recorded in Japanese on February 25, 2021
in the Special Lecture Hall of Happy Science in Japan
and later translated into English.*

In this chapter, there are a total of three interviewers from Happy
Science, symbolized as A, B, and C, in the order that they first appear.

1

Summoning the Guardian Spirit of Mr. Trump to Ask His Current Thoughts

The reactions of the Japanese media toward the new U.S. administration

RYUHO OKAWA

Today, we'd like to receive a spiritual message from Mr. Trump's guardian spirit for the second time this year. He hadn't come to us for a while, and the last time he came was just after his acquittal in his second impeachment trial. At that time, we recorded his spiritual message in my living room, so he expressed his wish to give another spiritual message in a more formal setting (see Chapter One of this book). Compared to the time when I was suddenly visited by Mr. Biden's guardian spirit in my bedroom, talking to Mr. Trump in my living room was certainly better. I think Mr. Trump's guardian spirit expressed most of his basic thoughts, but there are probably some unaddressed issues and questions we have to formally ask him.

It's only been a little over a month since the Biden administration took power. Looking at the general response of the Japanese media, they don't seem to have any particularly high expectations of Mr. Biden. They seem to be keeping an eye on how Mr. Biden will change Mr. Trump's ways. They are also watching whether the global coronavirus situation will drastically change with the use of vaccines and how the new administration will deal with issues regarding Burma (Myanmar), Hong Kong, and the Uyghur region.

The Japanese media's overall evaluation of him has been neither exceptionally positive nor negative. But the left-leaning mass media seem to be giving off a similar air to when the administration of Japan changed to the Democratic Party over a decade ago, after the Liberal Democratic Party lost. I sense that they are shaking Prime Minister Suga's footing quite a bit. So, it's possible for an era of confusion to come in the near future.

It seems the Japanese media honestly don't know what to say about Mr. Trump. During the 2016 election, everyone, including the Ministry of Foreign Affairs of Japan, had all agreed on Ms. Hillary Clinton taking a lead over Mr. Trump. But because the result turned out to be the complete opposite of their expectations, the Japanese media was shaken up. After the recent presidential election, too, the media seemed to be wondering whether the outcome would be overturned again, and were giving off an indescribable air.

However, Mr. Biden was gradually recognized as the new president after he started making contact with other world leaders. In addition, Mr. Trump made a speech near the U.S. Capitol Building calling on Republican supporters to walk down to the U.S. Capitol, and apparently, a number of people poured into the Capitol Building. The U.S. media portrayed this incident as a violent revolution, or a coup d'état, organized by the sitting president, and this also seems to have contributed to Mr. Biden being recognized as the new president.

Since then, Mr. Trump has settled in Florida and has been playing golf and spending time with his family. He's probably thinking about various things.

Happy Science published Trump-related books when others were silent

RYUHO OKAWA

Meanwhile, the Japanese mass media have been working hard behind the scenes to collect information in various ways. We were also approached by the major Japanese newspaper companies and TV stations who wanted to find out whether the opinions expressed by some of our members on YouTube and other social media sites represent the opinions of Happy Science.

Some of the far right-wing members of the U.S. Republican Party are considered to be blind or fanatic supporters of Mr. Trump, so the media are probably suspecting that the roots of their views could be found in Japan and are sniffing around for evidence. We have no intention of instigating people to hold such views, but I get the impression that the media are probing into the source of those views. We didn't hesitate to publish Trump-related books when others were silent, so I can understand why people may see us in that way.

Today, we have three interviewers here—two are proficient in English and one only in Japanese. I wonder which language I should use to conduct the spiritual interview. (The guardian spirit of) Mr. Biden used Japanese from the beginning, while (the guardian spirit of) Mr. Trump spoke in English at first. But recently, we have been able to conduct a spiritual interview with (the guardian spirit of) Mr. Trump in Japanese as well. So, what should we do? Interviewer B is of the highest rank among the three of you, so perhaps it's better to adjust our level to his vibrations [*laughs*].

I would feel bad if we interview Mr. Trump's guardian spirit in Japanese and he calls the Chief Director of International Headquarters (Interviewer C) an uncultured person. But I hope you will feel free to ask any questions.

OK. I will call him now.

The guardian spirit of Mr. Donald Trump. The guardian spirit of Mr. Donald Trump. [*While clapping.*] As promised, I am calling you today for our second interview—for a formal one. If there are any points you want to add, any messages you have for Mr. Biden and the others, or any comments for Japan or about world affairs, please tell us.

The guardian spirit of Mr. Trump, please come down here.

[*About 10 seconds of silence.*]

2

Mr. Trump's Honest Feelings After Leaving Office

"I feel that the 'Passion' has finally come upon me"

DONALD TRUMP'S GUARDIAN SPIRIT

Hmm, hmm...

A

Hello.

TRUMP'S G.S.

Ah, hmm.

A

Are you Mr. Donald Trump's guardian spirit?

TRUMP'S G.S.

Yes.

A

Thank you very much for this valuable opportunity today.

TRUMP'S G.S.

Well, this is where I must pay my respects to.

A

You have completed your four-year term as president, and looking back at those four years, they were quite full of ups and downs. But recently, it seems like the opportunities for you to express yourself have been taken away especially because your Twitter account (now called X) has been suspended. So, I think today is a truly valuable opportunity for you, too.

TRUMP'S G.S.

This might be a replacement for Twitter. Yes, maybe it is.

A

Yes, it's valuable in the sense that you can send your direct message to people all over the world.

TRUMP'S G.S.

Right. Word of mouth is my last resort. They won't let me use technology to express myself, so I have no way to share my thoughts other than to use this last form of media—word of mouth.

A

You have many fans not only in the U.S. but also in Japan. So, I think they are waiting to hear from you.

TRUMP'S G.S.

Oh, I have fans in Japan? That's good.

I sensed that you (Interviewer A) were supporting me. I wish I could have met your expectations.

A

Please don't worry about it.

TRUMP'S G.S.

You drew the short straw, didn't you?

A

No, I didn't.

TRUMP'S G.S.

So, you haven't been demoted yet?

A

No [*laughs*]. Well, it's not only about worldly matters.

TRUMP'S G.S.

Oh, is that so?

A

From a spiritual point of view, you showed us how a political leader should be, and it has been very educational for us.

TRUMP'S G.S.

I feel that the "Passion" has finally come upon me. Recently, I feel like I can understand how Jesus must have felt—just slightly. So, this is what it must have been like for Jesus.

Proud to have been the president of conviction

A

Frankly, how do you feel now? I'm sure you are also thinking a lot about your future plans.

TRUMP'S G.S.

Well, for four years, or I guess even longer, I continued to call the U.S. mainstream media "fake news" even while I was still the sitting president. That alone was miraculous. In that sense, I worked very hard. I believe I am worthy of being called "the president of conviction" for having never compromised my beliefs.

But after the new president took office, all of my achievements and contributions are starting to vanish, as if they are rapidly being buried in a sandstorm. To me, it looks like people are trying to erase my achievements and four years of a presidency from American history.

Regardless of whether I am the president, as a member of the force that makes up about half of the Congress, I believe I have to speak up and prevent the U.S. from heading in the wrong direction.

In the first place, it's wrong to undo everything the previous president did. Such a country could end up suffering from the so-called "British disease." At the time, the U.K. grew very weak because the Conservative Party and the Labour Party kept doing the opposite of what the other party did. Such things should not happen.

I actually have a lot to say, but if I say too much, apparently I sound too vulgar. So today, I want to make it appear as if I was tricked by your leading questions to say more than I had originally intended to say.

Suppression of free speech has revealed the presence of another power

A

While calling the media "fake news," you fought fair and square with your words. How do you view...

TRUMP'S G.S.

The U.S. is no longer a free country. On Twitter, I had 88 million followers around the world. Suspending my account and preventing me from tweeting is close to torture. It's like being in prison, don't you think? It's almost like that. I don't remember the U.S. being such a country.

Can't he fight words with words? I want to tell Biden to round up more than 100 million followers and fight back with words.

A

We have various topics to discuss separately, but taking a recent case, for example, there was an impeachment trial in the Senate. To be honest, I don't think that sort of thing should even be allowed.

TRUMP'S G.S.

I'm actually a little disappointed. I'm worried about Americans.

While I was still the sitting president, and despite that I was the sitting president, the media tried to make it look as if I were trying to gain control of the government through a coup d'état. It made me worry. Are they insane? There's something wrong here. The mainstream media probably believe they have the power to appoint the president.

But around the time they suppressed my speech, I think everybody saw that there exists a different power from the power of the people. This is an issue that must be overcome. We need to solve this issue for democracy to develop in a healthy way.

Back when the transportation system wasn't as convenient, newspapers may have been the only source of information people could rely on, but that's not the case now. Then who can correctly judge the integrated opinions of the infinitely diverse people in this world? This has become an extremely difficult challenge.

So, well, hmm... I get the feeling that things are heading toward chaos. You could call it diversity, but there's no unity in that idea alone.

I was portrayed like the military dictator of a certain country who took over the government by starting a coup d'état. But it was Biden, the president-elect, who mobilized the National Guard to defend the White House and the Capitol! It wasn't the sitting president. I wasn't the one who mobilized the military to suppress the opponents' speech.

So, it was quite strange. Really strange. Yes. I would say it's queer or weird.

A
Right.

There appears to be a kind of "madness" in the U.S.

A
The media and the Democratic Party all focused their efforts on attacking you since the beginning of your administration. They even suppressed the speech of the president. So, from the perspective of the Trump administration, you could say they were the ones who attempted a coup d'état.

TRUMP'S G.S.
At the very least, they started to suppress me while I was still the president, even before I left office.

A
Yes.

TRUMP'S G.S.
They also suspended my Twitter account. The question is whether that kind of power should be allowed in this world.

For example, the UN, which is headquartered in New York, would have no place to stay if the U.S. president decided to stop funding them and told them to leave. So, how is it possible for some people to prevent the sitting president from sending his messages to the citizens?

If this were to happen in Japan, it would be like all the media refusing to attend press meetings with Prime Minister Suga and ignoring all comments from him just because they don't like his opinions or because his son caused problems. If they only reported on the opinions expressed by the leader of the opposition party or broadcasted only the interviews with the Constitutional Democratic Party of Japan, for example, it would be strange, wouldn't it?

Based on what happened this time, I clearly understood that a kind of "madness" exists in the U.S. They probably viewed my side, or the group of "fanatic" Republicans, as insane. But from my perspective, I saw a kind of madness in the media, who believe themselves to be the world's "conscience." I believe only God can make a judgment on this matter.

3

The Change in Administration Will Divide America

The economic outlook based on Mr. Biden's budgeting and the fiscal deficit

A

Thinking about why such madness arose, it seems to have occurred not only from domestic issues but also foreign issues. You were actually confronting China directly through the trade war. So, it seems like everything happened in the course of those events.

TRUMP'S G.S.

Biden is trying to gain popularity in the first year of his presidency, so he allocated a large budget to fight the coronavirus. And the fiscal deficit has probably already reached tens of trillions of dollars. I think a major tax hike will come at some point, and the media will have to take the blame for it.

The fiscal deficit has increased so much because they (the Biden administration) want to make themselves look good to other countries and also because they have given up on having the U.S. restore its economy on its own.

I raised the energy issues as well, but instead of listening to what the U.S. president had to say, the media used the words of a Swedish teenage girl, who refuses to go to school, as the symbol of the UN. This really worries me.

If they are true adults, they should be telling her to go to school. Adults should be saying, "Go to school and graduate before you talk about science," or "Go to university to study meteorology and other subjects." But instead, they used her words to their advantage. This kind of trend—this frivolous tendency—is disappointing.

Objections to people labeling him as a "divider"

TRUMP'S G.S.

Although it might have appeared like I didn't know much about politics, I actually had achieved great success both financially and in business management. So, I have a certain level of insight as an independent American adult. Despite this, the media tried to portray me as... well, I don't know what they wanted to say, but they tried to make me look like a frivolous, anti-intellectual person. They tried to label the president as an icon of anti-intellectualism, while they portrayed those writing for newspapers or holding the microphone in front of TV cameras as intellectuals.

Ultimately, the Biden side was trying to label us as "dividers" and tried to spread that impression globally while portraying themselves to be working hand-in-hand with others. They are taking after what Mr. Obama did skillfully—using beautiful words to fabricate a good impression of themselves. So, the true dividers are the ones trying to label us as "dividers"; they are trying hard to shut out the opinions of the Republican Party completely. That's division. They are trying to suppress the opinions of one side.

I didn't do that. I even supported some of the rallies run by Democrats and approved of them. If the rallies were held for a good cause, I acknowledged that they were good and encouraged them. So, I supported what I thought was right regardless of whether it was organized by Republicans or Democrats.

I think they are far more of a divider and a suppressor. Well, nothing can be done now because there is nobody who can integrate the different ideas.

The weird logic about the coronavirus

A

There was already a movement to prevent you from getting reelected during the election campaign in 2020, but I assume you had some confidence in your chances of winning.

TRUMP'S G.S.

Well, this coronavirus was a little, you know... Even now, Biden is claiming in a grave manner that more than 500,000 Americans have died (at the time of this spiritual message) and that this death toll is higher than all past wars combined, including WWI, WWII, the Vietnam War, the Korean War, the Iraq War, and the Gulf War. In this way, he makes it sound like I've killed tons of Americans.

It's true that many Americans were killed. But instead of accusing the criminals who killed them, he is putting the blame on the president who was in office at the time of the killing and insisting that that's why he deserves to be the next president. I find this logic weird. If your cavalry units were completely destroyed by Native Americans, you should be shooting at the Native Americans who attacked them. But according to Biden, firing the military commander in chief who was in charge of the cavalry units is considered a victory. I think he is out of his mind.

A

Right. In a lecture held right after the U.S. presidential election, Master Ryuho Okawa said that the coronavirus pandemic is actually a "virus war" and that Biden's victory would mean the defeat of America rather than the victory of the Democratic Party.

TRUMP'S G.S.

That's what I thought.

Now, the Democratic administration is conducting human rights diplomacy and expressing concerns on the issues of Hong Kong and the Uyghurs. They are also putting pressure on Burma by denouncing the coup d'état as if to say that the U.S. hasn't changed. But from the very beginning, Mr. Biden banned the use of terms like "Wuhan virus" and "China virus" because using such phrases will lead to the discrimination against the Chinese people and other people of color, the yellow race, or Asians. To use the earlier example, this is as if the president is saying anybody who badmouths Native Americans will be punished even though Native Americans were the ones who attacked the cavalry units.

Criticizing Mr. Biden who thinks each country should be responsible for the pandemic

TRUMP'S G.S.
There would be no problem if an investigation were properly conducted and China were proven to be completely innocent. But it hasn't been proven yet. The WHO team went to China, but they couldn't do anything, right?

A
Right.

TRUMP'S G.S.
We all knew that from the beginning. How can there be any

evidence one year later? While the WHO team was under the two-week quarantine, China discussed and arranged everything behind the scenes, including what to show.

So, I was right when I said WHO is not functioning. They are useless. That's why I said the U.S. will stop funding them and leave. But the average person couldn't understand my decision.

He (Biden) is making it look like he's running ahead, when in fact he is lagging several laps behind me. The moment he issued an executive order banning the use of terms such as "China virus" and "Wuhan virus" at the start of his administration, he surrendered. So, he no longer has any enemies.

It is as if he is saying everybody—and every country—should understand that the coronavirus spontaneously occurred in each respective location and accept the situation as such. He is saying the president or the prime minister of the countries suffering high rates of infections and casualties must take responsibility for his or her lack of administrative abilities by resigning and having somebody new replace him or her. But to be blunt, that's like a "masochistic view of history," isn't it? I can only imagine Biden was Japanese in his past life.

A

Yes, he does seem to have a rather un-American attitude...

TRUMP'S G.S.

You should thoroughly research him. It's strange. What he says is very strange. Hmm, I find it weird. He's probably the reincarnation of some Japanese person who got shot down at the start of WWII. He was probably some nameless Japanese person who never accomplished anything and who nobody knows about. He's very suspicious.

A

What's more, Vice President Kamala Harris is a bit suspicious, too.

TRUMP'S G.S.

There's no need for you to hold a spiritual interview with her.

A

Oh, OK.

TRUMP'S G.S.
She probably doesn't have anything to say.

A
I see.

TRUMP'S G.S.
She only looks the part.

"China's tendency to lie is unacceptable as a developed country"

A
When you came here about two weeks ago for an informal spiritual interview (see Chapter One), you clearly stated that the People's Liberation Army of China is involved in the coronavirus issue.

TRUMP'S G.S.
I'm sure about that.

A

Yes, that's what you said. So, can you clearly say...

TRUMP'S G.S.

Ordinary people can't handle the virus, so the military forces that handle biological and chemical weapons must have been involved. China has special forces, so I'm sure those special forces did it. The consequences of an attack are clear once it happens, but it's difficult to anticipate the attack ahead of time. China has a considerable number of forces like that.

I really hate their tendency to lie! I myself make it a principle to be honest. I've been criticized so much because I'm an honest man. But China lies as a nation. It is unacceptable for a developed country to have such a tendency—or even for such country to exist. It's unacceptable.

A

The other day, you also said if someone is responsible for all that happened, that person should clearly be held accountable (see Chapter One). I assume you meant the leader of the nation.

TRUMP'S G.S.

Well, there's no way they would admit to it. The claims they make are unbelievable. For example, they claim that the virus issue would lead to the discrimination of China or that China was attacked by some other country.

The U.S. suffered a death toll of 500,000 people already, right? And the number of infected people is approaching 30 million (at the time of this spiritual message). But the number of infections in China doesn't reach 100,000 no matter how much time passes, and their death toll is even smaller. The actual number of cremation urns is very different from the reported number, but such lies can remain unchecked. Even if somebody speaks out about it, the evidence will immediately be erased. Once the corpses are all buried, nothing will be found. I don't think they should be allowed to become a world leader as they are now.

Apparently, Japan's former Prime Minister Abe also recognized that this is a world war, but he didn't have the courage to publicly announce it. The Japanese media don't have the guts to accept it, either. Japan doesn't have the confidence to voice such a view to the rest of the world; they are too weak to withstand China's verbal counterattacks or even the accusations by the Chinese press secretaries. So, well... somebody has to keep fighting.

It's really frustrating. Maybe I'm responsible for being disliked. But considering that I still got nearly half the votes despite the media denouncing me, I don't think the American people have been completely brainwashed. I think many people have been silenced in the current headwind. Well, this is a fight—a fight over the sense of value on Earth.

The purpose behind China's push for a Democratic administration

B

I have a question regarding the coronavirus. Some people say China is responsible for creating and spreading the coronavirus throughout the world and starting the pandemic. And as time passes, researchers involved are gradually starting to confess the truth, and some are beginning to testify or blow the whistle. A scientist who was awarded the Nobel Prize in Physiology or Medicine has also pointed out that, based on the analysis of the genetic structure, the coronavirus couldn't have been produced naturally, and concluded that it was man-made.

When you were the president, you clearly mentioned that you had evidence to support this claim. I'm sure an extensive investigation was conducted to collect information behind the scenes. So, what made you believe that China was the culprit?

TRUMP'S G.S.

Well, the U.S. has a significant amount of evidence. But now that the Democratic administration has started, the CIA and FBI are no longer disclosing the evidence they have. That was exactly what China was aiming for—to prevent this kind of evidence from coming out by pushing for a Democratic administration.

B

So, that was their purpose?

TRUMP'S G.S.

Yes, that's the reason why China was working so hard over a span of one year.

B

I see. So, they attempted to wipe out the evidence from the root?

TRUMP'S G.S.

Yes. That's why they needed a change in administration.

B

Was it their goal to wipe out evidence through a change in administration, then?

TRUMP'S G.S.

Yes, they thought they would be in trouble if the administration didn't change. So, they achieved their goal. The U.S. media didn't act according to their conscience but instead went after profits.

There is evidence. But it won't come out because everybody—not only the top-level politicians but also the officials—were replaced. There was a complete reshuffling in all the departments. Many people are moving in and out now. This is how our country is. I'm not sure if it's a good thing or a bad thing. In Japan, even if there is a change in administration, the officials remain the same, so it's different. In that sense, the U.S. isn't as consistent.

I'm sure information that is disadvantageous to Biden will not surface for the time being. But it might come out later on if there is greater pressure to remove him from office.

"The U.S. is a federation of states with different laws"

C

It appeared as if the U.S. media supported China this time. In addition, I got the impression that the judicial authorities did not demonstrate their sense of justice and made many decisions that were not backed by justice. Even from the perspective of the separation of powers, it seems like American democracy is no longer functioning. How do you feel about that?

TRUMP'S G.S.

Well, the situation is a bit different from Japan. America is the "United States"—it's a federation made up of a collection of "states." So, each state is like a country. Laws vary from state to state, and the courts can hand down different rulings depending on the state.

The difference between states goes beyond being a red state or a blue state. This is the Democratic Party's catchphrase, but depending on whether a state is a red or a blue state, it can become like another country. Although the U.S. is based on the rule of law, what is considered good or bad differs from state to state. That's what is so difficult about it.

Of course, we have the Supreme Court, but they are too lenient. They can judge whether something is constitutional or not, but they can't say much about what to do based on the laws of each state. So, even the judges are like politicians.

The six powers that can give influence on the U.S.

A

There have been a lot of speculation about the significant amount of illegal votes in the states where the Democratic Party is strong.

TRUMP'S G.S.

I'm sure there were [*laughs*]. But they are all working together to pretend no irregularities ever happened. They're working to seal everything away, as if plastering over a wall.

I am as good as "detained" in Florida, and they seem to be trying to destroy the properties I own while I'm unable to leave Florida. They are quite the conspiring organization.

A

I agree.

The U.S. is considered to be the leader of democratic nations, but if the election is proven to have been unfair, then the grounds for this idea will be shaken. What are your thoughts on that?

TRUMP'S G.S.

You (Interviewer C) just mentioned the separation of powers, but the legislature, executive, and judiciary are not the only powers. Journalism functions as the fourth power and Hollywood as the fifth.

In addition to those five powers, foreign investors also have an influence as the sixth power. Depending on where they invest, the foreign investors can have strong control over certain companies and their stocks. So, even if they don't have the right to vote in the U.S., they still have the power to influence the country because they have control over certain companies.

Well... they say I divided the country, but I was the one who tried to unify this divided country. Now, the Biden administration is trying to divide the country up again and break up what I tried to unify.

A

I have the impression that the American trait of decentralization of power worked negatively this time.

TRUMP'S G.S.

You're right. But it's actually quite strange how certain drugs are legal in some states and illegal in others. Or how committing a particular crime results in a death sentence in one state but not in another. It's quite unfair that the rules are different in every state. But the tax rates can also differ, and that's why some states are able to attract residents.

The U.S. is not as unified as Japan may think. It's a bunch of independent states. If you don't like the state you live in, you can just move to another state you prefer. If your views differ too much from the state's views, you can move to a Republican state or a Democratic state. If you don't like the mainland, you can move to Hawaii or Alaska. So, it isn't so easy to run this country, indeed.

4

Mr. Trump's Concerns Over the Shameful Side of America and the Future of Japan

Predictions on how Mr. Biden will close the criminal investigation against himself

B

Former President Trump, when you were in office...

TRUMP'S G.S.

When I hear "former," I feel weaker.

B

Oh, I'm sorry. But I must address you accurately.

TRUMP'S G.S.

I still feel like I'm the president.

B

I understand.

When you were in office, you sent out a strong message, "Make America Great Again." I think you tried to lead the country toward unification, not division.

Now that Mr. Biden has become the new president, what do you have to say about the future of America? Some say that the nation will decline under "strategic patience" or that the U.S. will rapidly fall from its position as the most powerful nation in the world.

Happy Science has also conducted much spiritual research, and based on the different views of various high spirits and space beings, we've concluded that President Biden is essentially a "great mediocre person."

TRUMP'S G.S.
"Mediocre person?" You shouldn't use such an honorific title.

B
Oh, is that so? I'm sorry.

TRUMP'S G.S.
I think he's a bit less than mediocre.

B

I see. So, the U.S. chose a mediocre person as the president. This could mean that he, as a populist, will increasingly be influenced by the people around him or start making blunders in various political decisions because of his mediocrity.

In your earlier spiritual message, "Trump Shall Never Die," recorded on February 18, you hinted that the Biden administration may become full of corruption.

TRUMP'S G.S.

I think it is already full of corruption. But now that he has taken control of the government, he will probably stop all criminal investigations against himself.

B

I see. So, you think Mr. Biden will stop the criminal investigations against himself.

TRUMP'S G.S.

Yes, he'll stop them by not allocating the budget. He can tighten the FBI budget. The FBI should have been carrying out a criminal investigation against him, but he will probably put a stop to it.

Instead, he is now trying to investigate every possible crime I might have been involved in. There is an infinite number of ways to frame somebody, and it's an underhanded method. You know, it's just like those covert operations that were practiced in Japan during the Edo period, when the country was controlled by shogunate spy groups. The U.S. is actually still living in such old times.

More people are expecting Mr. Trump to come back

B

With regard to that point, you mentioned earlier that you saw a power different from the power of the people.

TRUMP'S G.S.

Information is also a weapon. It's not always fair. It's a matter of how to use it as a weapon.

C

Even so, I think the Americans will not stay quiet once they become enraged by something they find unfair. What's more, some say that your current approval rating is higher than it was before the election.

TRUMP'S G.S.

Yes, it seems so. With every passing day, since about a month after the election, there have been more and more people expecting me to come back.

C

The CPAC (Conservative Political Action Conference) will be held in Florida soon.

TRUMP'S G.S.

Well, I don't know if the way the media cover the news is actually objective and fair. But I feel sorry for my supporters because the media are using the incident where people stormed into the Capitol as a perfect excuse to accuse them. If the media report that everybody who participated in the incident would be on the wanted list, Trump supporters would only look like bad people, or like escapees from the Sing Sing Correctional Facility, wouldn't they? It's like they have declared to arrest all Trump supporters who have strong faith in him and put them on a nationwide wanted list.

But what about the Democratic Party? Many incidents have occurred at different times, including looting supermarkets, murder, and rape. It's all a matter of how they are reported by the media.

So, hmm... Well, it's really frustrating. It seems like my supporters have been put in a disadvantageous position now, but I'm planning to make a counterattack at some point.

"Biden's camp is planning to divide the Republican Party through bribery"

A

Earlier, you said the media and financial powers have a lot of influence on U.S. politics. But regarding the last election in particular, the Democrats weren't the only suspicious ones; the Republicans were also wavering a bit and trying to decide which side to stand on. In Georgia, for example, even with a Republican governor, there was suspicion of the election being rigged. How do you view this situation? In terms of future plans, when thinking about the election in four years...

TRUMP'S G.S.

Well, some people want to be the president themselves. They are probably calculating whether it would be more advantageous for them to continue supporting Trump or whether they would have a greater chance under a new president. So, I think it's natural for them to waver between the two sides. I'm sure there are some who want to be president among those who served me, too.

Even if some people say, "Given that Biden became president at his age, Trump can run for president again in four years," others will say, "No, no, there are others who have potential." So, there is a plan to divide the Republican Party through this difference in opinion. This plan has been set up by Biden's camp, and they are trying to bribe some Republicans, in a sense.

Pointing out that the American media is headed toward totalitarianism

A

There are various kinds of information circulating on the Internet, including things the mainstream media do not cover. Some sources on the Internet say, for example, that there have been bribes in states with Republican governors, or that China has direct influence in some states. There are many similar stories like this. What are your thoughts on such situations behind the scenes? In other words, people are pointing out that American democracy is being undermined by foreign interference.

TRUMP'S G.S.

Well, I think China is desperate. They were being driven into a corner by me, and now they're trying to strike back. But it's like a mouse biting a cat's nose.

Nevertheless, my lawyer, former New York City Mayor Giuliani, and FOX TV, which was slightly more favorable toward me, are being sued for billions of dollars. This is crazy, no matter how you look at it.

It makes me want to ask, "Where is the freedom of the press?" or "Are you seeking totalitarianism?" If that were the case, we wouldn't need so many TV stations. We would just need to pick one and close the rest.

I'm sure people will calm down sooner or later, though. The U.S. is a "belligerent" country [*laughs*], so it tends to do anything it wants when it gets mad. The last phase of my presidency certainly had a similar atmosphere to the Civil War.

C

The public's trust in the media is declining, and more people are following the news on the Internet. But some information on the Internet are now being restricted, causing the content to swing between right and left. Do you have any plans to create some kind of media?

TRUMP'S G.S.

Well, in fact, it's very strange that somebody who served as president must create new media to express his opinions. It was essentially the mainstream media's job to report them.

But now, GAFA and the others couldn't pass up the attractive, huge Chinese market and gave in to temptation; they are thinking about making their way into that market in the future. Even if the U.S. imposes economic sanctions on China, China is making direct investments in Asia and setting up various media strategies to lure those companies, saying that they can survive as long as they conform to China's media strategies. In this way, they are competing for a better position in the global market.

We will have to see if Mr. Biden can outsmart them. Actually, I've been holding back a little. While I'm holding back, I hope people will cool off a bit. I don't know if my work truly appeared to be so crazy, but people need to check whether a president who thinks it's crazy to revitalize American industries is crazy or not.

The Biden administration is about to create massive unemployment. They're going to cause a lot of unemployment, weaken the local industries, and destroy faith in "America's attractiveness"—the idea that you can be rich and affluent if you become a success. I think they are moving toward making America less attractive by gradually leveling out those appealing qualities—the qualities that make people want to immigrate to America.

In the end, money will probably flow to those who support what Biden says, and he will equalize people's economic level by force. That's how I see it.

The Trump administration strove to speed up vaccine development

C

According to the conservative radio program I was listening to this morning, Dr. Fauci's superior at the U.S. National Institute of Allergy and Infectious Diseases has acknowledged that the vaccine, which would have taken five more years to develop, was made in just one year through Operation Warp Speed, thanks to President Trump's efforts. However, no one is paying attention to this. Biden and Fauci are also ignoring it and are only talking about the distribution of the vaccines. Hearing this, I felt that they were very unfair.

TRUMP'S G.S.

Now, it already looks like Biden is the one distributing the vaccines to the world.

C

Yes, it does.

TRUMP'S G.S.

Hahaha [*laughs*].

A

It should have been recognized as an achievement of the Trump administration.

TRUMP'S G.S.

Haha [*laughs*]. Well, usually, you can't make a vaccine in one year. It takes several years. So, you could call it a rush job... or perhaps a patch-up job. But to start, I gave them one year to make anything that is effective. I don't know how much research they had done on the virus, so it may not be completely trustworthy. But I thought it would be better than nothing. It would at least have some kind of placebo effect; people will be comforted just from the thought of having some kind of "weapon."

Biden is taking advantage of the vaccine, but he also has to take responsibility for any adverse reactions or side effects that arise as a result. I won't be able to stand it if he considers the effect and side effects separately and says, "Trump is to blame for the side effects." He must take responsibility for both the positive and negative outcomes.

The U.S. seems to have exposed their shameful side even before they could reform China. It's a bit disappointing. There's no way China would want to become a parliamentary democracy after seeing this. If anything, it probably made China become more determined to be a monolithic government.

Mr. Trump's views on the media making a fuss over the coronavirus

A

Does this mean that the outcome we see now is a little different from the plan you originally had?

TRUMP'S G.S.

Hmm. Right now, the world is only talking about the number of infections spreading, but you should subtract the number of people who have been discharged from the hospital. People have actually been cured. The media really likes to make a fuss. It's fun and work for them, so the number of deaths and inpatients has been their major concern. But the point is that there are also people who have been cured.

Everybody probably thinks that once they are infected, it's game over. But Prime Minister Johnson of the U.K., for example, is now back in office after having once been in the ICU. I was infected too, but I managed to leave the hospital in about three days.

I think the coronavirus is actually quite similar to measles or influenza in a way, although people may say this view is an unscientific or anti-intellectual way of thinking. You can't help being infected and it can't be prevented. But even if you get infected, you can get better and become immune to it. So, I think people are making far more fuss than they should.

It would be unbearable if the president or prime minister were replaced every time the flu spreads to millions of people. It may not have been every year, but the flu has spread to millions of people once every few years in various countries. So, it should not be such a big problem if you're used to it. But this time, nobody was used to the coronavirus, so it became a big deal. I myself got out of the hospital right away and showed how I was refusing to lose to such a virus. And I think there are actually a lot of people like that.

It's the basic habit of the mass media to only report on bad news. They're all like airport detection dogs that have been solely trained to sniff out the bags carrying drugs and to bark loudly at them. They've been trained to find only these "bad things" and only react strongly to them.

It's probably the same in Japan. After receiving and listening to the constant reports on the coronavirus over the last year, half of your brains must have gone crazy. You wouldn't have this problem if you don't watch the news. But people these days watch TV and read the newspaper, and they also spend many hours a day on their smartphones on average. That's how their minds keep getting "polluted." They don't have to do any of that, but they easily get the urge to do so.

I think we need to bring back a little more peace and order into this world. There seems to be a trend of frivolous information forming too many "whirls" or international public opinions. People don't have the eyes to look intently at what is essential.

The prospective outcome of the
Biden administration's "human rights diplomacy"

A

I think President Trump's supporters and fans are hoping that you will continue to fight until the bitter end. Do you have any thoughts on your future plans?

TRUMP'S G.S.

For the time being, Biden is distributing money, so it may feel like money is raining down from the heavens. Under these circumstances, people probably won't complain. But because the government is running a budget deficit, they will have to figure out how to make up for the money that was distributed. The question is how to deal with this problem.

A

Also, ever since it became clear that President Trump was leaving office, there have been signs of the world situation changing drastically in many places. There was a political upheaval in Myanmar, democratic activists in Hong Kong are getting arrested, and China is increasing its pressure on Taiwan.

TRUMP'S G.S.

Well, that's actually the nature of what they call "human rights diplomacy." Mr. Obama received the Nobel Peace Prize soon after he became president because he advocated a world without nuclear weapons in his speech. But in reality, he didn't reduce the number of nuclear weapons and instead worsened the situation; he allowed China to expand and become more powerful in terms of the economy and the military. He also worsened the relationship with North Korea. So, reality is very different.

In reality, I, who didn't win the Nobel Peace Prize, met with Kim Jong-un to make sure that nuclear weapons would not be used. So, Japan is in greater danger now that I have stepped down as president. Anything could happen at any time, and China is posing a greater threat. Those who don't see this situation as dangerous are the ones who are called "mediocre people."

Although it may be due to a sense of nostalgia, the leftists in Japan truly and fundamentally like the idea of equal poverty or equal slavery that comes from oppression or dictatorship. They don't seem to understand what it really means. They don't understand that it's the same as equality in prison. Rather than raising such an issue, a lot of people wish to destroy the Trump Tower and believe that the world would be more peaceful if they could relieve their grudge in that way. But if they were to knock down the Trump Tower, their thoughts would be no different from those of the Muslims who destroyed the World Trade Center.

"Japanese politicians don't know how to have a proper discussion"

A

I'm sure you had some interest in the political situation in Japan as well. Although it may have been difficult for you to clearly state your opinions while in office, I think you can be frank with us now and tell us what Japan should do. Do you have anything to say about Japan?

TRUMP'S G.S.

Hmm… Speaking from the perspective of an outsider, you seem to be having a hard time. Mr. Suga seems to be struggling, and a tough situation will continue even after he leaves office. Well… when I think about the future of Japan, it's very depressing.

I think you guys should merge with the state of Hawaii. It might be safer that way.

A

Are you suggesting that Japan should seek protection from the U.S. in that way?

TRUMP'S G.S.

Hmm. You are covered under the U.S.-Japan Security Treaty, but you never know what might happen, so you should probably be annexed. Don't you think you'd be able to get along with Hawaii and become one country?

A

Do you mean Japan doesn't look like it has the power to fight on its own?

TRUMP'S G.S.

Well... [*laughs*] Looking at Japan in its current state, you will be finished while the politicians are having a discussion. They don't know how to have a proper discussion in the first place. Instead, they are busy tripping each other up. They accuse others of being entertained or for being involved in a scandal. It was funny to hear that eating out and drinking at night, eating steak with a group of people, or drinking alone at a bar is enough reason for the politicians to get fired as part of taking responsibility.

Japan is such an interesting country [*laughs*]. Really... In some ways, it's really interesting. It feels like I'm reading *Gulliver's Travels*. It's like this island country is governed by ants, and the ants are making a fuss over various things. Although Japan makes a fuss over trivial matters, when Chinese public vessels enter the waters around the Senkaku Islands or when those ships have been reinforced with armaments, they cover very little in the news and won't even discuss what to do. That's just how the country is. It's a very strange country.

5

How to Deal with China's Repeated Human Rights Abuses

China, which uses human beings as a means to an end, needs a "surgical operation"

B

Ever since Mr. Biden took office, there have been some drastic changes in America's relationship with China in particular. There have also been reports on how Mr. Biden's views on human rights issues, or on human rights diplomacy which was brought up earlier, greatly differ from yours.

In a telephone call with Mr. Xi Jinping on February 10, 2021, Mr. Biden made some statements that appeared to defend China's human rights violations as a product of Chinese culture. He said, "There must be a united, tightly controlled China, and Xi Jinping uses his rationale for the things he does based on that," and "Culturally, there are different norms that each country and their leaders are expected to follow," hinting that such conducts cannot be avoided. There have been reports on how these comments provoked a strong backlash from people across the U.S.

In contrast, Mr. Trump raised the North Korean abduction issue at the UN for the first time as the U.S. president, although this is not widely known in Japan. You also successively passed the human rights bills for the Uyghurs, Tibet, and Hong Kong to counter China's suppression of human rights and tried to stop China's reckless behaviors. In this way, you have been setting the tone for developed countries.

Now that the views on human rights have completely changed from the previous administration, what kind of relationship do you think Mr. Biden is going to have with China?

TRUMP'S G.S.

I think his logic is the same as saying, "People must have had various reasons to import many black slaves from Africa." You could justify slavery in many ways, by saying for example, "Given the circumstances at the time, they had no choice," "They probably wanted cotton workers. It couldn't be helped because the cotton business was necessary," or "They needed to use those slaves as a replacement for cattle and horses." You could also say, "The Egyptian Pharaohs had no choice but to use farmers to build the pyramids."

These reasons may have been true, but basically, the purpose of modern democracy is to realize the happiness of each individual. So, it is fundamentally wrong to use human beings as a means. Despite this, China clearly holds the idea of using humans as a means to an end. They basically don't see any problem with burying 100 million people under Tiananmen Square, for example, if it means protecting the Communist Party, or more specifically, protecting the leadership, or even more specifically, protecting Xi Jinping. Abiding by the law created by the central executive committee is more important to them. I think many people misunderstand this point.

In fact, their law is a law that benefits the ruler. They have no qualms about sacrificing the lives of their own people for the sake of preserving the law. And should foreign countries interfere, China will thoroughly lash out at those countries and even try to cause them some damage. I think China needs a "surgical operation."

B

A "surgical operation"?

TRUMP'S G.S.

Yes. We must do what we didn't do at the time of the Tiananmen Square incident—or what we couldn't do because of Japan.

"Humans cannot control global warming"

C

The first thing that the Biden administration did was to halt oil production, overturn the Keystone XL Pipeline project, and make Mr. John Kerry an envoy to show that the U.S. is participating in the fight against global warming. Meanwhile, it snowed in Texas, where it's usually warm.

TRUMP'S G.S.

Ha [*laughs*].

C

It seemed like it was a punishment from heaven. Then, there was a major power outage as well.

TRUMP'S G.S.

That was funny. No, I shouldn't say funny because I'm not entirely excused from taking responsibility for what happened.

There was a huge snowstorm in Texas. Icicles were falling from the spinning ceiling fans and sea turtles were freezing. People had to pull tens of thousands of sea turtles onto land to warm them up. Oh, "global warming" is a serious problem. It brings snow, kills sea turtles by freezing the ocean, and causes icicles to hang from fans that are supposed to cool us down. This is global warming, huh? It's a serious problem. Yes, I thought it's serious, indeed.

In Japan, too, when people were intently speaking out about global warming, it snowed heavily, and many cars were stranded on the road for days. As you said, I also think the Will of God is telling us that we are making a mistake. Somebody like me who has a vague, though not perfect, understanding of God's Will can sense the meaning of such events, but those who are far from this level can hardly grasp why these things are happening.

Global warming isn't something that can be controlled by the amount of CO_2 emitted by mere humans. It isn't like a flame on the stove—it really isn't. Global warming is caused by the periodic changes in the amount of activity of the magma inside Earth and the periodic activity of the Sun's flares. We already know from the past that these factors influence the occasional alternations between periods of warming and cooling. This is scientifically understood from the past data. But if we try to artificially "control" global warming by warning each other, "Don't grill mackerel! Then, we can stop global warming!" it will only lead to bloodshed on both sides.

The job of politicians at a time of crisis caused by climate change

TRUMP'S G.S.

It's been about 10,000 years since the Ice Age ended, so it isn't so easy to know what kind of era lies in the future. In the past, there were some places that sank into the ocean, but there were also lands and mountains that surfaced. There is nothing we humans can do about the great will or movement of this Earth as a whole.

If areas near the coasts sink, we just need to build towns closer to the mountains. It's as simple as that. If it gets too cold, people should move to the warmer areas. There is no other choice. Such instances have occurred many times in history. Cities developed, but after they were ruined, these civilizations moved to another area. This has happened many times in the past. We can't do anything about it.

If Ms. Greta's home country Sweden becomes buried in snow—though it's always been covered with snow—and gets too cold to stay there, she can move to the Mediterranean. She could live there instead. Or, she can go to Africa, and Africa may become civilized. Things like this have happened many, many times in the past.

I feel sorry for Japan. It is said that a large percentage of the world's volcanoes are concentrated on these tiny islands of Japan, although I forget how many. I don't know the exact percentage, but at the very least, I think Japan has about 10 percent of the world's volcanoes. A significant amount of the world's volcanoes is concentrated on this small Japanese archipelago which makes up less than one percent—only a fraction of a percent—of the world's total area. This means that a time may come when a volcano explodes with a *bang*, blows up the country into pieces, and forces everybody to flee to sea on rafts. The Japanese civilization was built in such a dangerous place.

But I think nothing can be done about it. If such a time does come, you have no choice but to move to another place. It is the job of the politicians to negotiate with Putin and ask him to let you live somewhere in Siberia where the permafrost is thawing. So, I think this issue is beyond the efforts of individuals.

What should have been done at the time of the Tiananmen Square incident?

A
Earlier, you said something important about the Tiananmen Square incident. You said there is something that should have been done then and that needs to be done now. What did you mean by this? You are here as a guardian spirit now, so I think you can frankly speak to us about what you think.

TRUMP'S G.S.
What happened in the Soviet Union should have properly been done in China as well. Information should have been

disclosed, and what exactly happened should have been reported. With regard to the human rights issue, the names of the victims and the people who died should have been announced at the very least.

Furthermore, they should have shown a complete, accurate video footage of the incident. But in reality, they only showed part of the footage and hid the rest to make the damage look very small. Some say only 30 or so people were killed, while others say 3,000 were killed. Countries like the U.K. says 10,000 people died at the time.

China has the habit of covering things up like that in no time. In that country, those who exercise freedom of press are immediately arrested or sentenced to death.

At the time of the Tiananmen Square incident, information should have been disclosed. The West may have assumed that China had joined the Western Bloc, but they should have noticed that China under Deng Xiaoping's leadership, which they were trying to support, had not changed at all in its nature.

The U.S. and Europe more or less condemned China, but not Japan. The Japanese central government at the time happened to be dominated by politicians who felt guilty for Japan's alleged past behaviors that led China to suffer. There were many politicians who thought like that; Kiichi

Miyazawa, Yohei Kono, and Tomiichi Murayama to name a few. In no time, they concluded that the Tiananmen Square incident was nothing compared to the atrocities committed by the Japanese military during WWII and quickly decided that Japan would not impose economic sanctions on China. They even had the Japanese emperor visit China at China's request and conducted something similar to "panda diplomacy."

This appeared to have improved the relationship between Japan and China, but in the end, it was Japan that fell into a trap. Afterward, Japan suffered great economic downfall, and China rose to great power and made strides to become a military superpower. Japan failed to read such trend ahead of time. If China had been given a strong warning at that time, I assume the trend of the world would have been very different.

A
Right.

What will Mr. Biden do if the U.S. fleets come under Chinese attack?

A

Some say the Chinese Communist Party regime should have been liberalized when the Soviet Union dissolved. Now, the world is tackling the issue of how to confront the authoritarian regime run by the Communist Party of China. Do you have any plans on how to do that?

TRUMP'S G.S.

It seems like Biden has sent some U.S. fleets near China, but the question is what he will do if those ships truly come under Chinese attack. It's worth watching. I, too, want to see how he will react. What will he do? China has already made weapons that are strong enough to attack U.S. aircraft carriers, so I'd like to know what he will do about them.

Now, other countries are staying vigilant and keeping an eye on the Spratly Islands and the Paracel Islands. But China is also aiming to take the Pratas Islands. This is something the Japanese are unaware of, right? These islands are located off the west coast of Taiwan. China is planning landing operations there. Even if these islands were taken by China, Japan will not... If you look at these islands from Japan, they are located behind Taiwan, so they might not seem to have anything to do with Japan. But if China manages to occupy these islands, Taiwan may be left to deal with the matter on their own. So, it's a serious problem.

Once China successfully takes these islands, they will take over various other places as well. The other islands aren't safe either because China is a country that reclaims islands from the sea to build military bases. The same goes for the Senkaku Islands. If China sends many vessels equipped with weapons to the Senkaku Islands, makes a landing, and builds a fortress in three days, then those islands would be effectively controlled by China. It will become like Takeshima Island. I wonder what Japan will do.

If Japan has enough power to take those islands back on their own, then Japan deserves to form a military alliance on equal footing with America. But if Japan just begs America to do something about it, we have to say, "Wait a minute. If you are not willing to do anything yourselves, why should Americans attack and take back those uninhabited islands, or the islands actually inhabited by the Chinese?" This is a logical way of thinking, isn't it? Of course, the U.S.-Japan Security Treaty applies, but it doesn't mean the U.S. promised to win back the occupied islands.

I don't know if China is all talk or if they will truly take action. I'm sure they will make a few provocative moves this year, but the question is whether they will actually take action.

Furthermore, China is also bullying Taiwan right now. They are trying to prevent Taiwan from getting vaccines. They are not giving Taiwan any vaccines and are also putting pressure on European countries to reject all of Taiwan's requests for vaccines. They are trying to cut off supplies completely to isolate Taiwan.

Can Biden deal with these matters? I would like to see what he'll do. I think Japanese politicians will probably be slow to react.

A

Right. Having you as the U.S. president was very important for the Japanese people as well. I think we can say that you were the best president.

6

The U.S. Should Bear Responsibility for the World

The true meaning of "America First"

A

You spoke to us the other day too, so if you have any final comments you need to say to the people of the world, please share them with us. Are you waiting for the public to start calling out for Trump?

TRUMP'S G.S.

Well, apparently my words are "too harsh" and they seem to evoke a lot of negative reactions if I say too much. That's why I'm thinking of lying low for a while.

Biden may be willing to show his working ability for a year or two, much like what Isoroku Yamamoto did. But his administration will eventually reveal their weakness because their policies lack consistency. In the meantime, we have to gather more people to side with us and gradually turn the public opinion around.

You know, people must not misunderstand the meaning of "America First." It means that the U.S. should be responsible for the world. So, we must maintain our power to take responsibility for the world. One source of this power is economic power. The other source of power is the ability to make decisions and take action. We must have these powers.

There are people who chose him (Mr. Biden). Although fake votes and votes from dead people were also counted, with those votes included, 80 million people voted for Biden. Ghosts might also have the right to vote, so I can't deny that. The "votes from ghosts" might have been included, but I want those 80 million people to take a closer look at whether they voted for the right candidate.

On the Chinese traditional idea of divine punishment

TRUMP'S G.S.

Democracy has never existed in China. Although pro-democracy movements have occurred in China recently, democracy has never taken root or succeeded in modern-day China. They have always been ruled by emperors or kings.

However, even if the nation was governed by a king or emperor, they had a belief since ancient times that such ruler was sent from heaven. But even heaven can make mistakes from time to time. So, whenever there was a bad emperor, people believed that they could give him divine punishment.

If people think heaven made a mistake, they could inflict divine punishment and start a revolution to found a new dynasty. They believed this to be in accordance with the will of heaven. This worked like democracy in an era when there was no election system. In the old days, there were peaceful transfers of power by abdication, of course.

In any case, people believed it accorded with heaven's will to carry out divine punishment whenever there was an evil king or a ruler who was seemingly possessed by a devil. I believe something occurs to keep the balance.

For countries that don't believe gods exist, I believe we need to prove them wrong. Well, Xi Jinping isn't immortal. He has many enemies close by. I think there are people around him who are aiming to punish him on behalf of heaven. There are people who are attempting to change China even if it means they'll end up dying with him. So, I'd like to watch what will happen within China.

"If the Reagan administration had another term..."

TRUMP'S G.S.

It's all right for the U.S. president to have term limits, but there are also bad things about it. Reagan served two terms and resigned at that age, but if he had served another term, things might've turned out differently after the Tiananmen Square incident. It's unfortunate.

We should've reconsidered the two-party system as well. The American people tend to judge things based on their image. After Bush Sr. won the Gulf War, he lost the election because of a live broadcast of his "vomiting incident" in Japan. The Americans then chose the younger Clinton, but Clinton tried to weaken Japan and strengthen China. That's one of the reasons we are now being beaten by China.

"People haven't been able to philosophically clarify what is wrong with communism"

TRUMP'S G.S.

People haven't been able to philosophically clarify what is wrong with communism. After all, this is what we are saying: "The word *equality* sounds nice, but if it means equality among slaves, we have to reject it. If all white people are made into black people because all people must be equal and it's not right for there to be a difference between black and white people, then we can't accept such equality." We can't accept it. We are saying, "We won't accept the kind of equality that says, 'The problem is that there are white people. Black racism is not good. Let's paint white people's faces with black ink and treat them the same way.'"

I think it's a good thing to open up a new path for black people, but pushing for equal results alone is wrong. It's impossible for African countries and the U.S. to become equal. There are about 1.3 billion people in Africa, so if we were to distribute our wealth to the African people, who live on one percent of the American people's income, to realize equality, the American people would lose over half of their property at that point. That would be very harsh for Americans. That means the African people would get income they didn't earn, while the American people would suddenly lose their property. This actually happened under the Miyazawa administration in Japan. It happened in broad daylight.

We believe we shouldn't conduct politics in such a way that allows people's hard work go to waste. We believe we must give the gospel of success to those who strive in accordance with God's Will. We don't believe that equal result for all is always a good thing.

I would like to add that although it's fine to try to make yourself look good, you shouldn't say things you can't do, and you shouldn't do things that will deprive people of their hope in the future of humanity.

A
Thank you very much.

Create a "spiritual community" between Japan and the U.S., and form a U.S.-U.K.-Japan alliance to share common values

A

Mr. Trump was the kind of leader who could sense God's Will very clearly.

TRUMP'S G.S.

I have faith, you know. Biden really doesn't know who God is. He doesn't even know the difference between God and paper (God and paper are both pronounced "kami" in Japanese), but I feel God. That's why I'm here, talking to you.

So, let's create a "spiritual alliance" between Japan and the U.S. somehow. OK?

A

Yes.

TRUMP'S G.S.

I hope we can create an alliance among the people who can understand the Will of God. I'd like to have at least one such base in Asia, one in the West, and another in Europe.

Now, regarding the Hong Kong problem, the U.K. is saying they'll accept 5,000 Hong Kong people into their country because they feel responsible. Having experienced Brexit, they probably feel a little isolated, so they'll come to us. Let's try to form a kind of alliance, at least among the U.S., U.K., and Japan, so that we can share common values.

I don't want to hear any more about Blue States, Red States, or bringing the two together. I'd like us to adopt God's mind as our own and be equal under our belief in God.

You guys have advanced teachings. You should spread them to the world. Just as some people in Japan claim you are fanatic and blind believers, so will some people in the U.S. Their arguments contain a "materialist trap." They always bring up "this-worldly comfort." You must not lose to that.

A

I understand. Thank you very much.

"Do what you think is right, regardless of the political party you support"

A

[*To the other interviewers*] Any other questions?

TRUMP'S G.S.

Well...

A

We, too, would very much like to be leaders to realize that.

TRUMP'S G.S.

Yes. [*To Interviewer A*] I'm glad you didn't lose your position. Keep it up, and try a little harder.

A

We will continue to support you.

TRUMP'S G.S.

Uh-huh. OK.

A

We hope you will continue to speak out and take action.

TRUMP'S G.S.

You translated a book supporting the Republicans, so I was worried that you might've been fired already.

A

Actually, I thought the book was a necessary guideline for the world. Before the Japanese people could get to it, you presented an example as a political leader.

TRUMP'S G.S.

[*To Interviewer C*] As you manage International Headquarters, you will probably meet supporters of both the Republican Party and the Democratic Party through your activities, but you must tell them to do the right thing regardless of which party they support. "Do what you think is right." OK? That's what you should tell them. You should also tell them to always watch out for the biases of the mass media.

I never once have thought of making money by becoming the president. I just wanted to make use of my talents. I wanted to make use of them for America and the world. If I just wanted to make money, I'd be better off working in real estate. We couldn't really carry out economic activities, so we had much loss, financially speaking.

If Biden were much younger than me, I wouldn't be able to say much, but since he is older than I am, there's much more... He probably underestimated me just because I'm younger, so I think I need to work a little harder.

Well, Japan is the most... Biden seems to suspect that some people in Japan are spreading something similar to the "conspiracy theory" that Trump and the "fanatic, blind supporters" of the Republican Party believe in, so he's checking up on Happy Science. But being targeted by them (the Biden administration) means Happy Science is a movement run by people whose intentions are closest to God's Will.

A
It is the right opinion, not a "conspiracy theory."

TRUMP'S G.S.
That's right. Yes, yours is definitely the right opinion.

A

Japan is the epicenter because Master Ryuho Okawa is in Japan.

"The true purpose of democracy is to build a nation of God"

TRUMP'S G.S.

If Hong Kong dissolves, people of Hong Kong will have to flee to the ocean. If they will be arrested even on ships or airplanes, they can only swim away, but then, they might either get caught or get shot from helicopters or drones. Even if they could make it to Taiwan, Taiwan itself might be surrounded (by Chinese forces).

I want to ask the people who voted for Biden, "Can he really prevent such a situation?" They probably hadn't even thought about it. After all, it's something that would happen on the other side of the globe for them.

Protecting the democratic system itself is not what's important. The purpose of democracy is to guarantee people's right to live happily, and its true purpose is to build a nation of God. The real mission of politicians is to realize God's justice in this world and to reflect the kingdom of

God in heaven onto this world, even a little. We have to tell this to people.

People have become too materialistic in their thinking, so I don't like it very much. In the U.S., people say they won't be infected by the coronavirus if they wear two masks, but if they don't cut it out, they'll die from suffocation. If older people wear two masks and go for a jog, they will really die from breathing difficulties.

A

Yes. You, President Trump, were the embodiment of justice, so we would like to continue to be hopeful of your future.

TRUMP'S G.S.

Maybe you guys suffered damage because you supported me, but I'm very glad to know that there are voices of support, even from Japan. It's very encouraging. There are other people praising Biden, so that should be enough. I'm thankful that you're proving there are still intelligent, sane Japanese people out there.

"I believe I will make a comeback someday"

A

Thank you very much for your valuable time today.

B

Thank you very much.

TRUMP'S G.S.

Biden's tax hike is dangerous, so it must be crushed.

A

That's true.

TRUMP'S G.S.

I'm serious, it's dangerous. Who knows what will happen after that? Japan is also in danger. If the vaccine doesn't work, what will come next?

A

There might come an economic depression. It's very likely.

TRUMP'S G.S.

The (Japanese) stock prices are rising, but it's very suspicious.

A

There can also be political confusion...

TRUMP'S G.S.

The only reason the stock market is bullish is because there's a money glut. Maybe people think that Japan has suffered less damage compared to other countries and are expecting everything to get better. But this year will be a crucial year, even for Japan. Whether or not Japan will sink into a bottomless pit again will depend on this year.

The Happiness Realization Party seems to have been ignored by mass media, just like me, but I hope they will keep on fighting. It was unfortunate that I couldn't support them as you had hoped.

A

We still count on you, and we wish you the best.

TRUMP'S G.S.

Trump shall never die.

Trump forever.

Trump will come back.

Like a phoenix and like Jesus Christ, Trump will rise again.

Yes, he will.

The day will come.

I believe so.

A

Yes. Thank you very much for your valuable message.

TRUMP'S G.S.

Sure.

7

Be Brave and Send Out the Right Opinions, Fair and Square

RYUHO OKAWA

[*Claps once.*] That was him.

I guess it takes courage just to publish a book like this in Japan. Anyway, we shouldn't be cowardly. We supported Mr. Trump when he became the president and while he was in office. We also insisted that Japan should adopt his reforms into its politics. So, we don't intend to run and hide without taking responsibility for what we said just because he lost the election.

We weren't plotting anything. We've always sent out the right opinions, fair and square. Even in a lecture at Saitama Super Arena, I said the right things, fair and square, so we're not hiding anything (see "With Savior," the lecture given at El Cantare Celebration on December 8, 2020). We should say what we think is right.

The people of Asia might have to suffer a great tragedy from now on, and the American people who have been working very hard to achieve success until now might suffer a huge tax hike.

Japan is no different. Ms. Greta is advocating so-called "carbon totalitarianism," and even Prime Minister Suga has jumped on the bandwagon and is considering a "carbon tax." He wants a reason to impose taxes. It means anyone who emits carbon dioxide will be taxed. We're not surrounded by a swarm of mosquitoes, so the tax offices are scarier.

Carbon itself is neither good nor bad. Used well, it will turn into a diamond, but used poorly, it will become charcoal. That's all.

People who are quick to jump to such an unscientific and short-sighted conclusion are probably driven by their emotions. But I would like people to remain calm.

A

Yes. Thank you very much.

RYUHO OKAWA

Well, it seems like we can't get Mr. Trump's help right away, but we should keep doing what we must.

A

Yes. Thank you very much for today.

RYUHO OKAWA

OK [*claps once*].

Afterword

Mr. Trump is an honest and bold man. In that sense, he is trustworthy.

The Japanese government is working hard to make sure the U.S. Biden administration affirms that the Senkaku Islands fall under the scope of the Japan-U.S. Security Treaty. This is the best they can do; they remain weak in the face of China and are only sending out their usual, ambiguous messages.

If the Japanese Ministry of Foreign Affairs were like the Chinese Ministry of Foreign Affairs, it would certainly declare that "The Senkaku Islands, Hong Kong, Taiwan, and surrounding areas are Japan's core interests," that "Japan will build a manned defense base to protect the Senkaku Islands," and that "In case of an emergency in Taiwan and Hong Kong, Japan has the duty to take the lead in protecting pro-democracy groups that have faith." It is also natural for Japan to think about protecting Myanmar's democratic forces and strengthening alliances with Australia, the U.K., and India.

British Prime Minister Johnson has announced his decision to increase the cap on nuclear warheads from the current 180 to 260 in response to the situation in Hong Kong. This is a Trump-like approach.

Now, the world needs leaders who can think about world justice. This must be the Will of God.

Ryuho Okawa
Master & CEO of Happy Science Group
March 17, 2021

ABOUT THE AUTHOR

Founder and CEO of Happy Science Group.

Ryuho Okawa was born on July 7th 1956, in Tokushima, Japan. After graduating from the University of Tokyo with a law degree, he joined a Tokyo-based trading house. While working at its New York headquarters, he studied international finance at the Graduate Center of the City University of New York. In 1981, he attained Great Enlightenment and became aware that he is El Cantare with a mission to bring salvation to all humankind.

In 1986, he established Happy Science. It now has members in 171 countries across the world, with more than 700 branches and temples as well as 10,000 missionary houses around the world.

He has given over 3,500 lectures (of which more than 150 are in English) and published over 3,150 books (of which more than 600 are Spiritual Interview Series), many of which are translated into 42 languages. Along with *The Laws of the Sun* and *The Laws of Hell*, many of the books have become best sellers or million sellers. To date, Happy Science has produced 27 movies under his supervision. He has given the original story and concept and is also the Executive Producer. He has also composed music and written lyrics for over 450 pieces.

Moreover, he is the Founder of Happy Science University and Happy Science Academy (Junior and Senior High School), Founder and President of the Happiness Realization Party, Founder and Honorary Headmaster of Happy Science Institute of Government and Management, Founder of IRH Press Co., Ltd., and the Chairperson of NEW STAR PRODUCTION Co., Ltd. and ARI Production Co., Ltd.

BOOKS BY RYUHO OKAWA

Personal Growth Titles

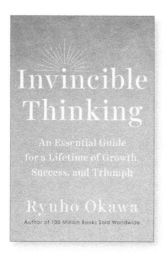

Invincible Thinking

An Essential Guide for a Lifetime of Growth, Success, and Triumph

Hardcover • 208 pages • $16.95
ISBN: 978-1-942125-25-9 (Sep. 5, 2017)

When we encounter adversity, hardship or failure, how can we find the resilience and will to persevere? On the other hand, what can we do when everything is going well for us? It is our mental attitude that determines whether we can realize continuous growth and joyful achievement in any circumstance.

In this book, Ryuho Okawa lays out the principles of invincible thinking that will allow us to achieve long-lasting triumph. This powerful and unique philosophy is not only about becoming successful or achieving our goal in life, but also about building the foundation of life that becomes the basis of our life-long, lasting success and happiness.

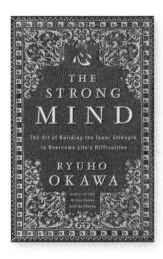

The Strong Mind

The Art of Building the Inner Strength to Overcome Life's Difficulties

Paperback • 192 pages • $15.95
ISBN: 978-1-942125-36-5 (May 25, 2018)

The strong mind is what we need to rise time and again, and to move forward no matter what difficulties we face in life.

In this book, Ryuho Okawa presents a self-transformative perspective on life's hardships and challenges as precious opportunities for inner growth. It will inspire and empower you to take courage, develop a mature and cultivated heart, and achieve resilience and hardiness so that you can break through the barriers of your limits. With this book as your guide, life's challenges will become treasures that bring lasting and continuous enrichment to your soul.

The Laws of Success

A Spiritual Guide to Turning
Your Hopes Into Reality

Paperback • 208 pages • $15.95
ISBN: 978-1-942125-15-0 (Mar. 15, 2017)

The Laws of Success offers 8 spiritual
principles that, when put to practice in
our day-to-day life, will help us attain
lasting success. The timeless wisdom and
practical steps that Ryuho Okawa offers
will guide us through any difficulties and
problems we may face in life, and serve
as guiding principles for living a positive,
constructive, and meaningful life.

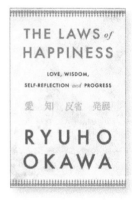

The Laws of Happiness

Love, Wisdom, Self-Reflection and
Progress

Paperback • 264 pages • $16.95
ISBN: 978-1-942125-70-9 (Aug. 28, 2020)

Happiness is not found outside us; it is
found within us. It is in how we think, how
we look at our lives, and how we devote
our hearts to the work we do. Discover
how the Fourfold Path of Love, Wisdom,
Self-Reflection and Progress creates a life
of sustainable happiness.

Worry-Free Living

Let Go of Stress and
Live in Peace and Happiness

Hardcover • 192 pages • $16.95
ISBN: 978-1-942125-51-8 (May 15, 2019)

The wisdom Ryuho Okawa shares in this book about facing problems in human relationships, financial hardships, and other life's stresses will help you change how you look at and approach life's worries and problems for the better. Let this book be your guide to finding precious meaning in all your life's problems, gaining inner growth and practicing inner happiness and spiritual growth.

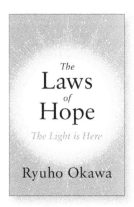

The Laws of Hope

The Light is Here

Paperback • 224 pages • $16.95
ISBN:978-1-942125-76-1 (Jan. 15, 2021)

This book provides ways to bring light and hope to ourselves through our own efforts, even in the midst of sufferings and adversities. Inspired by a wish to bring happiness, success, and hope to humanity, Ryuho Okawa shows us how to look at and think about our lives and circumstances. By making efforts in your current circumstances, you can fulfill your mission to shed light on yourself and those around you.

El Cantare Trilogy

The Laws of the Sun, the first publication of the Laws Series, ranked in the annual best-selling list in Japan in 1994. Since then, the Laws Series' titles have ranked in the annual best-selling list every year for more than two decades, setting socio-cultural trends in Japan and around the world. The first three Laws Series are *The Laws of the Sun*, *The Golden Laws*, and *The Laws of Eternity*.

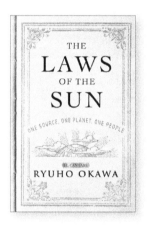

The Laws of the Sun

One Source, One Planet, One People

Paperback • 288 pages • $15.95
ISBN: 978-1-942125-43-3 (Oct. 25, 2018)

IMAGINE IF YOU COULD ASK GOD why He created this world and about the spiritual laws He used to shape us and everything around us. If we could understand His designs and intentions, we could discover what our goals in life should be and whether our actions move us closer to those goals or farther away.

At a young age, a spiritual calling prompted Ryuho Okawa to outline what he innately understood to be universal truths for all humankind. In *The Laws of the Sun*, Okawa outlines these laws of the universe and provides a road map for living one's life with greater purpose and meaning. In this powerful book, Ryuho Okawa reveals the transcendent nature of consciousness and the secrets of the multidimensional universe as well as the meaning of humans that exist within it. By understanding the different stages of love and following the Buddhist Eightfold Path, he believes we can speed up our eternal process of development. *The Laws of the Sun* shows the way to realize true happiness—a happiness that continues from this world through the other.

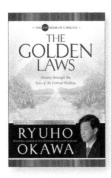

The Golden Laws

History through the Eyes of
the Eternal Buddha

E-book • 204 pages • $13.99
ISBN: 978-1-941779-82-8 (Sep. 24, 2015)

Throughout history, Great Guiding Spirits of
Light have been present on Earth in both the
East and the West at crucial points in human
history to further our spiritual development.
The Golden Laws reveals how the Divine Plan
has been unfolding on Earth, and outlines
5,000 years of the secret history of humankind.
Once we understand the true course of history,
through past, present, and into the future, we
cannot help but become aware of the significance
of our spiritual mission in the present age.

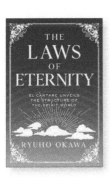

The Laws of Eternity

El Cantare Unveils the Structure of
the Spirit World

Paperback • 224 pages • $17.95
ISBN: 978-1-958655-16-0 (May 15, 2024)

"Where do we come from and where do we go
after death?"
This unparalleled book offers us complete
answers to life's most important questions that
we all are confronted with at some point or
another.
This book reveals the eternal mysteries and the
ultimate secrets of Earth's Spirit Group that
have been covered by the veil of legends and
myths. Encountering the long-hidden Eternal
Truths that are revealed for the first time in
human history will change the way you live
your life now.

Latest Laws Series

The Laws Series is an annual volume of books that are comprised of Ryuho Okawa's lectures that function as universal guidance to all people. They are of various topics that were given in accordance with the changes that each year brings.

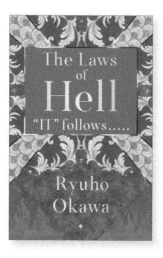

The Laws of Hell

"IT" follows.....

Paperback • 264 pages • $17.95
ISBN: 978-1-958655-04-7 (May 1, 2023)

Whether you believe it or not, the Spirit World and hell do exist. Currently, the Earth's population has exceeded 8 billion, and unfortunately, 1 in 2 people are falling to hell.

This book is a must-read at a time like this since more and more people are unknowingly heading to hell; the truth is, new areas of hell are being created, such as 'internet hell' and 'hell on earth.' Also, due to the widespread materialism, there is a sharp rise in the earthbound spirits wandering around Earth because they have no clue about the Spirit World.

To stop hell from spreading and to save the souls of all human beings, Ryuho Okawa has compiled vital teachings in this book. This publication marks his 3,100th book and is the one and only comprehensive Truth about the modern hell.

Recommended Books

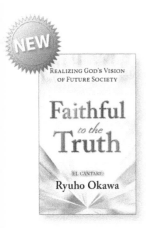

Faithful to the Truth

Realizing God's Vision of Future Society

Paperback • 164 pages • $20.00
ISBN: 979-8-887371-12-2 (Apr. 24, 2024)

The spiritual truth and the forecasts written in this book are messages from God that people worldwide should know right now. The world is on the verge of collapse. So, now is the time when people should listen to what Okawa is saying, as he is the one who knows the Truth, who can see God's vision, and who is trying to guide humanity in the right direction.

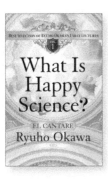

What Is Happy Science?

Best Selection of Ryuho Okawa's Early Lectures (Volume 1)

Paperback • 256 pages • $17.95
ISBN: 978-1-942125-99-0 (Aug. 25, 2023)

The Best Selection series is a collection of Ryuho Okawa's passionate lectures from the ages of 32 to 33 that reveal the mission and goal of Happy Science. This book contains the eternal Truth, including the meaning of life, the secret of the mind, the true meaning of love, the mystery of the universe, and how to end hatred and world conflicts.

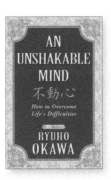

An Unshakable Mind

How to Overcome Life's Difficulties

Paperback • 180 pages • $17.95
ISBN:978-1-942125-91-4 (Nov. 30, 2023)

This book will guide you to build the genuine self-confidence necessary to shape a resilient character and withstand life's turbulence. Ryuho Okawa breaks down the causes of life's difficulties and provides solutions to overcome them from the spiritual viewpoint of life based on the laws of the mind.

Bestselling Buddhist Titles

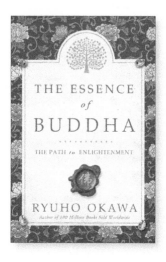

The Essence of Buddha

The Path to Enlightenment

Paperback • 208 pages • $14.95
ISBN: 978-1-942125-06-8 (Oct. 1, 2016)

In this book, Ryuho Okawa imparts in simple and accessible language his wisdom about the essence of Shakyamuni Buddha's philosophy of life and enlightenment—teachings that have been inspiring people all over the world for over 2,500 years. By offering a new perspective on core Buddhist thoughts that have long been cloaked in mystique, Okawa brings these teachings to life for modern people. *The Essence of Buddha* distills a way of life that anyone can practice to achieve a life of self-growth, compassionate living, and true happiness.

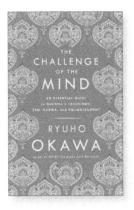

The Challenge of the Mind

An Essential Guide to Buddha's Teachings: Zen, Karma and Enlightenment

Paperback • 208 pages • $16.95
ISBN: 978-1-942125-45-7 (Nov. 15, 2018)

In this book, Ryuho Okawa explains essential Buddhist tenets and how to put them into practice. Enlightenment is not just an abstract idea but one that everyone can experience to some extent. Okawa offers a solid basis of reason and an intellectual understanding of Buddhist concepts. By applying these basic principles to our lives, we can direct our minds to higher ideals and create a bright future for ourselves and others.

The Challenge of Enlightenment

Now, Here, the New Dharma Wheel Turns

Paperback • 380 pages • $17.95
ISBN: 978-1-942125-92-1 (Dec. 20, 2022)

Buddha's teachings, a reflection of his eternal wisdom, are like a bamboo pole used to change the course of your boat in the rapid stream of the great river called life. By reading this book, your mind becomes clearer, learns to savor inner peace, and it will empower you to make profound life improvements.

Words of Wisdom Series

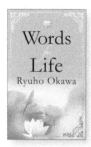

Words for Life

Paperback • 136 pages • $15.95
ISBN: 979-8-88727-089-7 (Mar. 16, 2023)

Ryuho Okawa has written over 3,150 books on various topics. To help readers find the teachings that are beneficial for them out of the extensive teachings, the author has written 100 phrases and put them together. Inside you will find words of wisdom that will help you improve your mindset and lead you to live a meaningful and happy life.

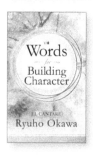

Words for Building Character

Paperback • 140 pages • $15.95
ISBN: 979-8-88737-091-0 (Jun. 21, 2023)

When your life comes to an end, what you can bring with you to the other world is your enlightenment, in other words, the character that you build in this lifetime. If you can read, relish, and truly understand the meaning of these religious phrases, you will be able to attain happiness that transcends this world and the next.

Words to Read in Times of Illness

Hardcover • 136 pages • $17.95
ISBN: 978-1-958655-07-8 (Sep. 15, 2023)

Ryuho Okawa has written 100 Healing Messages to comfort the souls of those going through any illness. When we are ill, it is an ideal time for us to contemplate recent and past events, as well as our relationship with the people around us. It is a chance for us to take inventory of our emotions and thoughts.

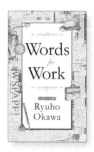

Words for Work

Paperback • 140 pages • $15.95
ISBN: 979-8-88737-090-3 (Jul. 20, 2023)

Through his personal experiences at work, Okawa has created these phrases regarding philosophies and practical wisdom about work. This book will be of great use to you throughout your career. Every day you can contemplate and gain tips on how to better your work as well as deepen your insight into company management.

MUSIC BY RYUHO OKAWA

El Cantare Ryuho Okawa Original Songs

A song celebrating Lord God / With Savior

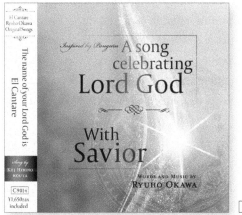

Words & Music by Ryuho Okawa

1. A song celebrating Lord God—Renewal ver.
2. With Savior —Renewal ver.
3. A song celebrating Lord God— Renewal ver. (Instrumental)
4. With Savior —Renewal ver. (Instrumental)
5. With Savior —Renewal ver. (Instrumental with chorus)

WHO IS EL CANTARE?

El Cantare means "the Light of the Earth." He is the Supreme God of the Earth who has been guiding humankind since the beginning of Genesis, and He is the Creator of the universe. He is whom Jesus called Father and Muhammad called Allah, and is *Ame-no-Mioya-Gami*, Japanese Father God. Different parts of El Cantare's core consciousness have descended to Earth in the past, once as Alpha and another as Elohim. His branch spirits, such as Shakyamuni Buddha and Hermes, have descended to Earth many times and helped to flourish many civilizations. To unite various religions and to integrate various fields of study in order to build a new civilization on Earth, a part of the core consciousness has descended to Earth as Master Ryuho Okawa.

Alpha is a part of the core consciousness of El Cantare who descended to Earth around 330 million years ago. Alpha preached Earth's Truths to harmonize and unify Earth-born humans and space people who came from other planets.

Elohim is a part of the core consciousness of El Cantare who descended to Earth around 150 million years ago. He gave wisdom, mainly on the differences between light and darkness, good and evil.

Ame-no-Mioya-Gami (Japanese Father God) is the Creator God and the Father God who appears in ancient literature, *Hotsuma Tsutae*. It is believed that He descended on the foothills of Mt. Fuji about 30,000 years ago and built the Fuji dynasty, which is the root of the Japanese civilization. With justice as the central pillar, Ame-no-Mioya-Gami's teachings spread to ancient civilizations of other countries in the world.

Shakyamuni Buddha was born as a prince into the Shakya clan in India around 2,600 years ago. When he was 29 years old, he renounced the world and sought enlightenment. He later attained Great Enlightenment and founded Buddhism.

Hermes is one of the 12 Olympian gods in Greek mythology, but the spiritual Truth is that he taught the teachings of love and progress around 4,300 years ago which became the origin of the current Western civilization. He is a hero who truly existed.

Ophealis was born in Greece around 6,500 years ago and was the leader who took an expedition as far as Egypt. He is the God of miracles, prosperity, and arts, and is known as Osiris in Egyptian mythology.

Rient Arl Croud was born as a king of the ancient Incan Empire around 7,000 years ago and taught about the mysteries of the mind. In the heavenly world, he is responsible for the interactions that take place between various planets.

Thoth was an almighty leader who built the golden age of the Atlantic civilization around 12,000 years ago. In Egyptian mythology, he is known as God Thoth.

Ra Mu was a leader who built the golden age of the civilization of Mu around 17,000 years ago. As a religious leader and a politician, he ruled by uniting religion and politics.

WHAT IS A SPIRITUAL MESSAGE?

We are all spiritual beings living on this earth. The following is the mechanism behind Master Ryuho Okawa's spiritual messages.

1 You are a spirit

People are born into this world to gain wisdom through various experiences and return to the other world when their lives end. We are all spirits and repeat this cycle in order to refine our souls.

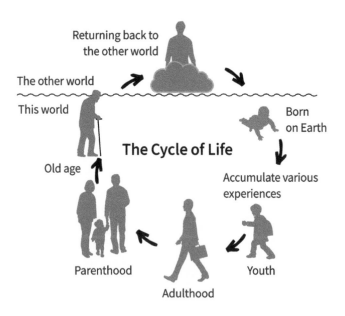

Returning back to the other world

The other world

This world

Born on Earth

The Cycle of Life

Old age

Accumulate various experiences

Parenthood

Adulthood

Youth

2 You have a guardian spirit

Guardian spirits are those who protect the people who are living on this earth. Each of us has a guardian spirit that watches over us and guides us from the other world. They were us in our past life, and are identical in how we think.

3 How spiritual messages work

Master Ryuho Okawa, through his enlightenment, is capable of summoning any spirit from anywhere in the world, including the spirit world.

Master Okawa's way of receiving spiritual messages is fundamentally different from that of other psychic mediums who undergo trances and are thereby completely taken over by the spirits they are channeling.

Master Okawa's attainment of a high level of enlightenment enables him to retain full control of his consciousness and body throughout the duration of the spiritual message. To allow the spirits to express their own thoughts and personalities freely, however, Master Okawa usually softens the dominancy of his consciousness. This way, he is able to keep his own philosophies out of the way and ensure that the spiritual messages are pure expressions of the spirits he is channeling.

Since guardian spirits think at the same subconscious level as the person living on earth, Master Okawa can summon the spirit and find out what the person on earth is actually thinking. If the person has already returned to the other world, the spirit can give messages to the people living on earth through Master Okawa.

Since 2009, many spiritual messages have been openly recorded by Master Okawa and published. Spiritual messages from the guardian spirits of people living today such as Donald Trump, Vladimir Putin and Xi Jinping, as well as spiritual messages sent from the spirit world by Jesus Christ, Muhammad, Thomas Edison, Mother Teresa, Steve Jobs and Nelson Mandela are just a tiny pack of spiritual messages that were published so far.

Domestically, in Japan, these spiritual messages are being read by a wide range of politicians and mass media, and the high-level contents of these books are delivering an impact even more on politics, news and public opinion. In recent years, there have been spiritual messages recorded in English, and English translations are being done on the spiritual messages given in Japanese. These have been published overseas, one after another, and have started to shake the world.

For more about spiritual messages and a complete list of books in the Spiritual Interview Series, visit okawabooks.com

ABOUT HAPPY SCIENCE

Happy Science is a religious group founded on the faith in El Cantare who is the God of the Earth, and the Creator of the universe. The essence of human beings is the soul that was created by God, and we all are children of God. God is our true parent, so in our souls, we have a fundamental desire to "believe in God, love God, and get closer to God." And, we can get closer to God by living with God's Will as our own. In Happy Science, we call this the "Exploration of Right Mind." More specifically, it means to practice the Fourfold Path, which consists of "Love, Wisdom, Self-Reflection, and Progress."

Love: Love means "love that gives," or mercy. God hopes for the happiness of all people. Therefore, living with God's Will as our own means to start by practicing "love that gives."

Wisdom: God's love is boundless. It is important to learn various Truths in order to understand the heart of God.

Self-Reflection: Once you learn the heart of God and the difference between His mind and yours, you should strive to bring your own mind closer to the mind of God—that process is called self-reflection. Self-reflection also includes meditation and prayer.

Progress: Since God hopes for the happiness of all people, you should also make progress in your love, and make an effort to realize utopia in which everyone in your society, country, and eventually all humankind can become happy.

As we practice this Fourfold Path, our souls will advance toward God step by step. That is when we can attain real happiness—our souls' desire to get closer to God comes true.

In Happy Science, we conduct activities to make ourselves happy through belief in Lord El Cantare, and to spread this faith to the world and bring happiness to all. We welcome you to join our activities!

We hold events and activities to help you practice the Fourfold Path at our branches, temples, missionary centers and missionary houses

Love: We hold various volunteering activities. Our members conduct missionary work together as the greatest practice of love.

Wisdom: We offer our comprehensive collection of books of Truth, many of which are available online and at Happy Science locations. In addition, we offer numerous opportunities such as seminars or book clubs to learn the Truth.

Self-Reflection: We offer opportunities to polish your mind through self-reflection, meditation, and prayer. Many members have experienced improvement in their human relationships by changing their own minds.

Progress: We also offer seminars to enhance your power of influence. Because it is also important to do well at work to make society better, we hold seminars to improve your work and management skills.

HAPPY SCIENCE'S ENGLISH SUTRA

"The True Words Spoken By Buddha"

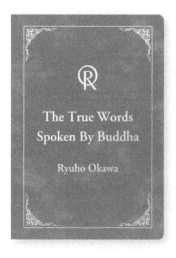

"The True Words Spoken By Buddha" is an English sutra given directly from the spirit of Shakyamuni Buddha, who is a part of Master Ryuho Okawa's subconscious. The words in this sutra are not of a mere human being but are the words of God or Buddha sent directly from the ninth dimension, which is the highest realm of the Earth's Spirit World.

"The True Words Spoken By Buddha" is an essential sutra for us to connect and live with God or Buddha's Will as our own.

MEMBERSHIPS

MEMBERSHIP

If you would like to know more about Happy Science, please consider becoming a member. Those who pledge to believe in Lord El Cantare and wish to learn more can join us.

When you become a member, you will receive the following sutras: "The True Words Spoken By Buddha," "Prayer to the Lord" and "Prayer to Guardian and Guiding Spirits."

DEVOTEE MEMBER

If you would like to learn the teachings of Happy Science and walk the path of faith, become a Devotee member who pledges devotion to the Three Treasures, which are Buddha, Dharma, and Sangha. Buddha refers to Lord El Cantare, Master Ryuho Okawa. Dharma refers to Master Ryuho Okawa's teachings. Sangha refers to Happy Science. Devoting to the Three Treasures will let your Buddha nature shine, and you will enter the path to attain true freedom of the mind.

Becoming a devotee means you become Buddha's disciple. You will discipline your mind and act to bring happiness to society.

✉ EMAIL or **☏ PHONE CALL**
Please turn to the contact information page.

☎ ONLINE member.happy-science.org/signup/ 🔍

CONTACT INFORMATION

Happy Science is a worldwide organization with branches and temples around the globe. For a comprehensive list, visit the worldwide directory at happy-science.org. The following are some of our main Happy Science locations:

UNITED STATES AND CANADA

New York
79 Franklin St., New York, NY 10013, USA
Phone: 1-212-343-7972
Fax: 1-212-343-7973
Email: ny@happy-science.org
Website: happyscience-usa.org

New Jersey
66 Hudson St., #2R, Hoboken, NJ 07030, USA
Phone: 1-201-313-0127
Email: nj@happy-science.org
Website: happyscience-usa.org

Chicago
2300 Barrington Rd., Suite #400,
Hoffman Estates, IL 60169, USA
Phone: 1-630-937-3077
Email: chicago@happy-science.org
Website: happyscience-usa.org

Florida
5208 8th St., Zephyrhills, FL 33542, USA
Phone: 1-813-715-0000
Fax: 1-813-715-0010
Email: florida@happy-science.org
Website: happyscience-usa.org

Atlanta
1874 Piedmont Ave., NE Suite 360-C
Atlanta, GA 30324, USA
Phone: 1-404-892-7770
Email: atlanta@happy-science.org
Website: happyscience-usa.org

San Francisco
525 Clinton St.
Redwood City, CA 94062, USA
Phone & Fax: 1-650-363-2777
Email: sf@happy-science.org
Website: happyscience-usa.org

Los Angeles
1590 E. Del Mar Blvd., Pasadena,
CA 91106, USA
Phone: 1-626-395-7775
Fax: 1-626-395-7776
Email: la@happy-science.org
Website: happyscience-usa.org

Orange County
16541 Gothard St. Suite 104
Huntington Beach, CA 92647
Phone: 1-714-659-1501
Email: oc@happy-science.org
Website: happyscience-usa.org

San Diego
7841 Balboa Ave. Suite #202
San Diego, CA 92111, USA
Phone: 1-626-395-7775
Fax: 1-626-395-7776
E-mail: sandiego@happy-science.org
Website: happyscience-usa.org

Hawaii
Phone: 1-808-591-9772
Fax: 1-808-591-9776
Email: hi@happy-science.org
Website: happyscience-usa.org

Kauai
3343 Kanakolu Street, Suite 5
Lihue, HI 96766, USA
Phone: 1-808-822-7007
Fax: 1-808-822-6007
Email: kauai-hi@happy-science.org
Website: happyscience-usa.org

Toronto
845 The Queensway
Etobicoke, ON M8Z 1N6, Canada
Phone: 1-416-901-3747
Email: toronto@happy-science.org
Website: happy-science.ca

Vancouver
#201-2607 East 49th Avenue,
Vancouver, BC, V5S 1J9, Canada
Phone: 1-604-437-7735
Fax: 1-604-437-7764
Email: vancouver@happy-science.org
Website: happy-science.ca

INTERNATIONAL

Tokyo
1-6-7 Togoshi, Shinagawa,
Tokyo, 142-0041, Japan
Phone: 81-3-6384-5770
Fax: 81-3-6384-5776
Email: tokyo@happy-science.org
Website: happy-science.org

London
3 Margaret St.
London, W1W 8RE United Kingdom
Phone: 44-20-7323-9255
Fax: 44-20-7323-9344
Email: eu@happy-science.org
Website: www.happyscience-uk.org

Sydney
516 Pacific Highway, Lane Cove North,
2066 NSW, Australia
Phone: 61-2-9411-2877
Fax: 61-2-9411-2822
Email: sydney@happy-science.org

Sao Paulo
Rua. Domingos de Morais 1154,
Vila Mariana, Sao Paulo SP
CEP 04010-100, Brazil
Phone: 55-11-5088-3800
Email: sp@happy-science.org
Website: happyscience.com.br

Jundiai
Rua Congo, 447, Jd. Bonfiglioli
Jundiai-CEP, 13207-340, Brazil
Phone: 55-11-4587-5952
Email: jundiai@happy-science.org

Seoul
74, Sadang-ro 27-gil,
Dongjak-gu, Seoul, Korea
Phone: 82-2-3478-8777
Fax: 82-2-3478-9777
Email: korea@happy-science.org

Taipei
No. 89, Lane 155, Dunhua N. Road,
Songshan District, Taipei City 105, Taiwan
Phone: 886-2-2719-9377
Fax: 886-2-2719-5570
Email: taiwan@happy-science.org

Taichung
No. 146, Minzu Rd., Central Dist.,
Taichung City 400001, Taiwan
Phone: 886-4-22233777
Email: taichung@happy-science.org

Kuala Lumpur
No 22A, Block 2, Jalil Link Jalan Jalil Jaya
2, Bukit Jalil 57000,
Kuala Lumpur, Malaysia
Phone: 60-3-8998-7877
Fax: 60-3-8998-7977
Email: malaysia@happy-science.org
Website: happyscience.org.my

Kathmandu
Kathmandu Metropolitan City,
Ward No. 15, Ring Road, Kimdol,
Sitapaila Kathmandu, Nepal
Phone: 977-1-537-2931
Email: nepal@happy-science.org

Kampala
Plot 877 Rubaga Road, Kampala
P.O. Box 34130 Kampala, Uganda
Email: uganda@happy-science.org

ABOUT HS PRESS

HS Press is an imprint of IRH Press Co., Ltd. IRH Press Co., Ltd., based in Tokyo, was founded in 1987 as a publishing division of Happy Science. IRH Press publishes religious and spiritual books, journals, and magazines and also operates broadcast and film production enterprises. For more information, visit *okawabooks.com*.

Follow us on:

f Facebook: Okawa Books

▶ Youtube: Okawa Books

𝓟 Pinterest: Okawa Books

◎ Instagram: OkawaBooks

🐦 Twitter: Okawa Books

𝓰 Goodreads: Ryuho Okawa

——— **NEWSLETTER** ———

To receive book-related news, promotions and events, please subscribe to our newsletter below.

🔗 okawabooks.com/pages/subscribe

——— **AUDIO / VISUAL MEDIA** ———

YOUTUBE

PODCAST

Introduction of Ryuho Okawa's titles; topics ranging from self-help, current affairs, spirituality, religion, and the universe.